CANADA IN THE GLOBAL VILLAGE

COURSE TEXT

Heather Menzies

Published by Carleton University Press Inc.
Printed and bound in Canada

Canadian Cataloguing in Publication Data

Menzies, Heather, date-
Canada in the global village : a video-based half-year Canadian studies course

Includes bibliographical references.
ISBN 0-88629-336-7

1. Technology—Social aspects—Canada
2. Communication and culture—Canada.
3. Transportation—Social aspects—Canada. I. Title.

T23.A1M45 1997 303.48'3'0971 C97-900935-9

Carleton University Press gratefully acknowledges the support extended to its publishing program by the Canada Council and the Ontario Arts Council. The Press would also like to thank the Department of Canadian Heritage, Government of Canada, and the Government of Ontario through the Ministry of Culture, Tourism and Recreation, for their assistance.

For

URSULA FRANKLIN

friend and mentor

ACKNOWLEDGEMENTS

This text is a distillation of all that I've learned from teaching this course over the past 12 years. So the first thanks go to my students, whose sometimes brilliant, and often provocative questions and comments contributed immensely to my understanding. I also want to thank Ursula Franklin, Robert Needham and Ken Pryke for helpful comments and suggestions as I was developing the course into this form.

Thanks also to Barbara Cumming for her creative genius in laying out this book, and for her witty good humour through all the tedious stages. A special thanks to Paul Heuthorst for the wonderful montage used on the front cover. And finally, thanks to my editor, Heather Sherratt, for a job well done, and quickly.

I am also grateful to Sylvia Van Kirk and to Watson & Dwyer, publishers, for permission to publish an excerpt from *Many Tender Ties.*

CANADA IN THE GLOBAL VILLAGE

TABLE OF CONTENTS

INTRODUCTION

WHAT THIS TEXT IS ABOUT, AND WHY YOU MIGHT BE GLAD YOU'RE READING IT

When you think of Canada and history, what images and facts come to mind? Maybe John A. Macdonald or Wilfrid Laurier as historical figures, or events like the War of 1812. Try Canada and geography now. You might be flooded with images: mountains, Prairies and, of course, the mighty river systems and the Great Lakes. Economics, and you might think of branch-plant industrialization.

Now try Canada and technology. Perhaps the Canadian Pacific Railway comes to mind, or the Anik satellite. Maybe the skidoo or some other invention: the Avro Arrow.

This text — and the 12 videos that accompany it — will connect the dots of these technological images, and fill in the larger picture. Hopefully, at the end, you will see Canada's history, geography, political economy and even the much-maligned notion of Canadian identity in a whole new light: a light showing how much technological systems and infrastructures have shaped or been shaped by these things. Hopefully, too, this light will help you better understand the possibilities for Canada and for human society generally in today's global village of multi-media digital communication.

Elsewhere, you will have learned to think about Canada, or society generally, through the lens of history and various historical agents; or through the lens of social groups and institutions such as the state or business. Technology has largely been seen as a subject for engineers, and ignored in other disciplines. Certainly it's not examined critically as a social construction embodying important values choices, and as an historical and social agent in its own right, fundamentally influencing public and private affairs.

This book is important because it fills that gap. At a time when the medium truly is the message — that is, when communication technology critically shapes the environment in which we live and work — it's useful to take these media seriously. Transportation and communication systems make things happen, while mass media and knowledge systems shape what we perceive and understand as true about those events. This has consequences for Canada both regionally and as a whole, as well as for our personal and national identity.

Here, you will learn to view Canada through the lens of these technologies. You will trace Canada's development as a series of technological projects — from fur-trading routes to canals, railways and telegraphs, from print and broadcasting systems to the information highway. And you will see how these in turn have shaped

Canadian society, culture and identity. You will be invited to discuss the views that technology embodies human progress or fosters dependency. You will also explore some of the less examined views associated with women, workers, and the First Peoples of this country.

When you are finished, you will have a critical understanding of technology, and of current trends in both the global digital economy and the global village of culture and communication. As an informed citizen, you will be able to ask critical questions about how multi-media and information technology is being used in local schools and businesses, hospitals and libraries. And as a learner, you will be able to bring this critical understanding of communication, media and other technologies into your particular area of study.

GUIDE TO THIS TEXT AS PART OF A HALF-YEAR COURSE

I originally wrote this text to serve as a core component of a half-year course by the same title. The course unfolds through 12 units clustered into four theme-modules, plus a transition. Each unit includes a video of approximately 55 minutes, a corresponding chapter in this text and some additional suggested readings. A brief commentary on each of the readings is included at the end of each chapter in this text.

The first module introduces some important building-block concepts about technology, and some of the philosophical ideas and ideals that have shaped different approaches to technology and its use. The module begins with a retelling of the story of the Canadian fur trade to show both the centrality of technological systems and infrastructures in shaping Canada, and the importance of critically understanding them.

The second module takes what you've learned about technology as a social construction, and applies this to understanding its powerful effects in shaping Canada's economic and industrial development. In this module, Unit 4 focuses on hydro power and railways and their importance in industrialization on a national and even multi-national scale. It also looks at what this means for economic nationalism and technological dependency. Unit 5 focuses on technological restructuring since the mid-1970s with the convergence of computers and communication technologies. It examines the information systems central to the shift from an industrial to a post-industrial economy, and the emergence of a global digital economy. This unit focuses particularly on what this means for people and for organized labour, and includes a lively panel discussion.

Between the second and third modules is a "transition" which is a hinge taking you from a discussion of technology in the political economy to a discussion of technology involved more in the construction of images, identity and culture. This unit introduces you to some of the thinkers whose critical insights on technology are discussed throughout the course. These are: Ursula Franklin, George Grant, Harold Innis and Marshall McLuhan. It begins with a brief overview of how technology has been depicted in the visual and literary arts.

The third module focuses exclusively on communication technologies, particularly those associated with the mass media, and on how these influence culture and identity. Unit 7 looks at the development of printing and its growth into mass-circulation newspaper chains and large, multi-national textbook publishers. Unit 8 looks at the recurring patterns associated with the development of radio, television and film and the kind of "public" that these have in turn created. Unit 9 looks at media and other information monopolies not just from the perspective of available choice, but also with a critical examination of how public taste and choice are shaped in the first place.

The final module tries to bring all the concepts and theoretical themes together in a three-part exercise in summing up. Unit 10 looks at the present and future of the unfolding global information society. It raises a number of critical questions about the institutional agents involved in building, running and managing the infrastructures and systems of this new digital environment, and explores these questions in a panel discussion involving some of Canada's leading communication theorists. Unit 11 takes that discussion and places it in the larger context of the earth's own living environment. Drawing from women's reflections on household economies, new reproductive technologies and the environment (eco-feminism), this program invites you to consider not whether the global village can sustain itself, but whether it can sustain life — life in the larger social and natural environment.

A final unit will review the themes of the course, and some of the most important material used to support and illustrate those themes. Hopefully this unit will help you prepare for the final exam.

While the focus is on the technologies that have brought Canada into the global village, the approach taken in examining these technologies is widely interdisciplinary. It's a mix of history, political economy, economics, communication theory, cultural studies plus some women's studies and environmental studies. Though some background in any or all of these subjects is helpful, none is essential.

COURSE FORMAT AND MATERIALS

I have structured the videos to stand on their own. However, I strongly suggest that you read each chapter of the text before watching each video. It might also be useful to re-read the text after watching the video. You probably should also read the Commentary on Readings at the end of each chapter before reading those texts.

The course materials were prepared so that you can work largely on your own. However, you should have ample opportunity to dialogue with the course instructor, teaching assistants and fellow students either through traditional seminars or electronic chat groups. To this end, I have suggested some discussion-starter questions throughout the text.

The videos were directed by an award-winning video artist, Rob Thompson, and represent compressed and visually enriched course lectures. They include archival film footage, photos and other illustrations, plus location and studio scenes with myself. Sometimes I bring others into the discussion, through interviews and panel discussions. Sometimes I speak directly to the camera. Each program ends with a wrap-up and questions for you to consider.

This text defines each concept discussed in the video and provides further background to and explanation of the unit themes. Definitions are highlighted, and a Commentary on Readings is included at the end of each chapter, along with a list of sources. I have posed some questions at the beginning of each module and chapter. These are intended to help crystalize the goals and objectives of each section. I pose some additional questions at the end of each chapter too. These are intended as discussion starters as well as to test your comprehension of the key concepts under discussion.

MODULE 1

BACKGROUND

This module gives you important background for understanding the emerging global village of instant digital connectivity, and the place of people and countries like Canada in it. The background includes some building-block concepts for thinking about technology, especially communication and transportation technology, not just as inventions or isolated systems, but as the infrastructure of a political economy that also critically influences culture and identity.

The module starts with a retelling of the story of the fur trade. It's a familiar story, about history and geography, economics and political science. But the story has seldom been told through the lens of the technologies involved, and the biases or values embedded in these technologies. In retelling the fur-trade story through that lens, Unit 1 will demonstrate why it's important to take technology into account. It will show how powerfully technology can influence social and political events, as values and institutional priorities are built into technological structures by institutional agents associated with its design and construction. It's especially important to think critically about the technologies associated with storytelling and the creation of knowledge and conventional wisdom; the latter assumes, for example, that the story of Canada *begins* with the fur trade.

Unit 2 goes into more detail on technology as a social construction, extending the concepts of technology as a tool and system with concepts such as holistic versus prescriptive technological practice. It also introduces the concept of discourse as an organized system of discussion and knowledge production, with subtle biases built into its design and conduct.

Unit 3 will probe more deeply into the intellectual context from which modern technology and technological practice have emerged. It will contrast traditional First Nations' approaches to science and technology with the Euro-centred philosophies of modern science, liberalism and utilitarianism. This program highlights the importance of world views and mind sets in shaping people's thinking on everything from what is and is not "technology" or what is and is not "development."

OBJECTIVES At the end of this module, you should know how to think critically about the technologies on your desk and in your home. You will be aware of how such concepts as scale influenced what you bought or didn't buy, or how much of what sustains your life has come to you through vast transportation and distribution systems. You will also have some critical understanding of the philosophies or mind sets at work in this vast technological network of production, distribution and consumption. You will also have a basic vocabulary for critically analyzing all the other technologies discussed in the course.

CHAPTER 1

"TECHNOLOGICAL SYSTEMS AND CANADIAN DEVELOPMENT": THE CASE OF THE FUR TRADE

OVERVIEW

There is some merit in dating the development of Canada as a modern political economy from the days of the fur trade. It's not so much that furs were one item in a long list of staple resource exports which for a long time were considered to be almost the central pillar of Canadian economic development. It's because the lines of transportation used to convey those furs to European markets were the lines along which future large-scale development followed. The railway system followed the water routes of the fur traders. So did telegraphy and even radio and television. In fact the whole business of uniting the geography of Canada into one political entity owed a lot to the Hudson's Bay Company's far-reaching system of transportation and administration, and the map-making abilities of its associates.

This unit introduces you to the various technologies that went into that system: canoes and York boats, snowshoes and toboggans, rifles and snares, trading goods and trading posts and, of course, trans-Atlantic sailing ships.

But there's more to technology than just these individual tools or structures. There's money and the organizations associated with providing that money. The Hudson's Bay Company shareholders financed the trading and transportation system according to their own terms — terms which protected their investments and ensured healthy returns on them. But these terms had consequences, introducing "biases" and "rigidities" to the company's expanding trade-support system. The Hudson's Bay Company's Royal Charter, embodying the institutional support of the crown, was also a significant influence.

This unit also introduces you to the idea that the stories we are told about Canada are not always unbiased. In fact, there are biases and rigidities at work here too. To help illustrate these, we will turn the frame around. We will consider the story of the fur trade from here instead of from there: here being North America and the perspective of Canada's first peoples; there being Europe and the perspective of the Hudson's Bay Company merchants. We will also briefly look at development from the perspective of the poor and middle-class emigrants who were Canada's earliest settlers.

OBJECTIVES

When you have completed this unit, you should be able to answer the following questions:

1) What were some of the technologies involved in the fur trade, and what integrated them into a system?
2) What makes a system rigid? What are some of the rigidities involved?
3) What's the connection between a large-scale system and a structural monopoly?

STUDYING THE FUR TRADE is important for two reasons. First, it illustrates how the bias of communication in the modern era — what Harold Innis called "the bias of space" — was built into the development of Canada by European entrepreneurs. The extensive transportation system associated with the Hudson's Bay Company and its rival, the North West Company, established an extensive pattern for Canada's further development from east to west. Equally, if not more importantly, these systems represented major investments in the business of transporting resources out of the country and bringing finished manufactured goods back in return. These weren't just investments of money, however. They were also investments of knowledge, skill and political-economic orientation and allegiance. Furthermore, there was an inertia associated with these vested interests. As circumstances changed, this inertia would bias or incline these interests to maintain the life of those systems and the path of development along the same lines. Thus, when fish or furs declined as a volume export staple, investors didn't say, "Okay, let's get out of international trade, and commit ourselves to developments centred here in Canada." They looked around for another marketable resource as a new volume export staple to keep their shipping lines full. Timber and wheat, for example, filled the bill.

The larger the initial system, the more important this systemic bias or inertia is. That's why it's important to study large technological systems as forces shaping development, almost as historical agents in their own right.

It's equally important to understand how they are represented in official Canadian history and what other perspectives, and other concepts of "development," were left in the shadow. The fur trade, therefore, is an important case study in the social construction of conventional wisdom as well as the social construction of technological systems and infrastructures of development.

TRANSPORTATION/COMMUNICATION SYSTEMS AS SOCIAL CONSTRUCTIONS The systems supporting the business of the Hudson's Bay Company can be broken down into several categories:

1) Transportation systems: These systems consisted of everything from sailing ships, canoes, toboggans and snowshoes in the early days to York boats, paddlewheelers and steamships in later years.
2) Exchange systems: This ranged from trade goods supplied by the Hudson's Bay Company, such as kettles, rifles, tobacco, cloth and rum, to the beaver and other animal pelts taken in exchange. It also included the terms of exchange and

relationships between trading parties which the company, with its vested interest in making good returns on its investments, always tried to make as *unequal* as possible. In other words, it tried to get the most furs for the least expenditure in trade goods, and tried to sell the furs at the highest possible price in the London fur markets. As Harold Innis noted in the concluding chapter of his classic, *The Fur Trade,* "The economic history of Canada has been dominated by the discrepancy between the centre and the margin of Western Civilization." In other words, unequal relations.

3) Administrative systems: These were perhaps the most important systems of all, in that they were crucial for running the Hudson's Bay Company as an integrated whole. This meant ensuring that all the incremental returns made along the way, such as carrying general freight on its boats, flowed back to the London head office of the Hudson's Bay Company. It included everything from hiring and payment policies of the Hudson's Bay Company, to detailed instructions on packing freight canoes and the food provided to voyageurs, to upgrading the transportation infrastructure by investments in paddlewheelers and other technologies.
4) Financing systems: This category dovetails with administrative systems, particularly from the perspective of attracting investors and of ensuring steady returns. The Royal Charter granted by King Charles II in 1670 gave the Hudson's Bay Company a virtual monopoly on trade in the Canadian Northwest, known as Rupert's Land. This was a powerful attraction to investors in the joint-stock company, offering a measure of stability in the volatile world of mercantile capitalism, or capitalism based on trading. A broad base of investor support, in turn, helped it operate on the extensive scale that it did.

> **P**eople often distinguish *tool* from *system* as a difference of scale. The tool is something hand held, such as a telephone, while the system is something bigger, such as a freeway or a financial management system. But the key difference between them is organization and control. The word "tool" implies that the technology is controlled by the user. "System" implies a prior degree of organization and external control. Specific material technologies (tools) are brought together in a pre-determined use, and are applied to purposes controlled by the organizer or organization. See Unit 2 for a further elaboration on these differences, particularly as *holistic* and *prescriptive* technologies.

The integrated systems of transportation, communication and administration associated with the Hudson's Bay Company were influential because they involved huge fixed investments. With their large vested interests, these systems encouraged market expansion. As they helped expand markets for Britain's modern market economy, they both served and applied the "bias of space" in the modern era, and led Canadian development down certain dominant paths.

BIAS OF SPACE AND THE BIAS OF COMMUNICATION IN THE MODERN ERA Canadian economic historian and communication scholar, Harold Innis, coined the term "bias of space" in his extensive and important study of technology and civilization. He theorized that civilizations embodied a bias either toward spiritual concerns — the ***bias of time*** — or toward material concerns — the ***bias of space***. By this, he meant a desire to control space, by military conquest, administrative control or market expansionism. He argued that the modern era was characterized by a strong orientation to space, specifically to turning physical space into private property — real estate, resources. In other words, commodities. Instead of capturing lands, its orientation was toward capturing markets and expanding market share. In one essay, he called this "the penetrative powers of the pricing system."

> **BIAS AND SYSTEMIC BIAS**
>
> The Oxford English Dictionary defines bias as "an inclination, leaning, tendency, bent; a preponderating predisposition *towards*; a predilection, prejudice."
>
> The emphasis on the word "towards" is important, especially in understanding how bias is built into technological systems and other seemingly neutral structures, giving them a dynamic bent toward some activities and uses rather than others. Bias is built in through the choices made in how technology is designed, and how relations are organized within the system, all of which reflect the values and priorities of those involved in the system's design and organization. Once the system is up and running, the biases operate in a seemingly deterministic and unchallengeable way, as *systemic biases.*
>
> "Any goal of the technology is incorporated a-priori in the design and [at that point] is non-negotiable."
>
> (Ursula Franklin, *The Real World of Technology*, p. 25)

Furthermore, Innis argued that technology, particularly transportation and communication technology, played a crucial role in applying this civilizational bias in daily life. It gave the pricing system its power to penetrate geographic and social space.

In perhaps his most important insight, he argued that technologies for crossing big distances quickly — what he called space-binding media of communication — embodied the dominant bias of space in the modern era, and fulfilled it. Eventually, the bias could transform the whole space of the planet (including outer space, cyberspace, and the inner space of genetics and biology) into commodities exchanged in one global market place.

However, Innis also argued that a healthy, stable society required a balance, even a dialectical tension, between the biases of time and space, and between institutions associated with each. He worried that the rigid monopoly scale of institutions associated with the space bias was moving modern society away from a healthy state of civilization toward what he viewed as an unhealthy state of empire.

It's helpful therefore to understand how transportation and communication infrastructures become rigid monopoly-scale systems in the first place.

RIGIDITIES OF HUDSON'S BAY'S SYSTEMS The subject of rigidities, and how systems, representing fixed investments of money, develop rigidities, is dealt with in one of the supplementary readings. (See *Commentary on Readings* at the end of this chapter.)

At the heart of the rigidities in the Hudson's Bay Company's extensive transportation systems there is one compelling fact. For everything else they might have accomplished, these systems were set up to make money. They were created as vehicles to seek out material that could be sold in European markets and to distribute materials (generally, finished manufactured goods) that could be sold to markets being opened up in new colonies like Canada. Another compelling fact was the scale of investment that was required to engage in this trans-Atlantic trade. Not only did it include all the ships and canoes and other space-bridging technologies stretching from London to the hinterland of Canada. It was also extensive in time, in that investors' money was tied up for a year and more while trade goods were sent out from London and furs were brought back in return.

As a result the system was rigid in some significant ways.

First, there were ***financing rigidities***. These hinged on the fact that a lot of money was tied up in fixed assets such as ships and trading goods. A lot of this money was overhead costs — that is, the basic infrastructure of ships, forts and other structures which had to be paid for, and maintained, whether trade was flowing through them or not. Yet the investors expected regular returns on their investments. This meant that the company administrators were pressured to keep expanding their trade, and on terms that would keep channeling financial returns to the English investors. The rigid requirements associated with how these huge investments were financed led to another form of rigidity: that of centralized control and administration. The company's overall operations had to be controlled centrally because satisfying its investors who had put money into the system as a whole was vital to its continued existence.

Unused capacity is another type of rigidity, stemming from financing rigidities. In essence, the financing imposed a rigid requirement that the system be operated at full capacity so as to generate steady returns to investors and also to finance further expansion of the system. If the system operates below full capacity, the vested interests involved in the system will tacitly dictate that something else be found to fill the gap immediately.

Harold Innis noted that the instability and insecurity of financing all this infrastructure building prompted more than the rigid imperative to generate regular interest payments for portfolio investors. It also prompted moves toward monopoly organization and a continued reliance on support from the state or the crown.

CONSEQUENCES OF THESE LARGE-SCALE RIGID SYSTEMS

In the Conclusion to *The Fur Trade in Canada,* Innis wrote that the instability of large-scale capital-intensive transportation systems associated with the fur trade inevitably led to monopoly organizations around it (see Box).

> "The increasing distances over which the trade was carried on and the increasing capital investment and expense incidental to the elaborate organization of transport had a direct influence on its financial organization. Immediate trade with Europe from the St. Lawrence involved the export of large quantities of fur to meet the overhead costs of long ocean voyages and the imports of large quantities of heavy merchandise. Monopoly inevitably followed, and it was supported by the European institutional arrangements which involved the organization of monopolies for the conduct of foreign trade." (Innis, 1970:390)

He was also saying that the state condoned or even supported monopoly-scale institutions like the Hudson's Bay Company. These large, centrally controlled commercial institutions served as useful instruments (or media) to enable countries like England to achieve their agendas of empire building around the world. Commercial corporations and related shipping systems served as media for imperial expansion.

As the Irene Spry reading should make clear, corporations achieve the status of a ***structural monopoly*** when the smallest indivisible unit of investment required to compete in a given field is so large that only two or three (in the case of an oligopoly) can afford the price of admission, or where one company completely dominates the field, in a total monopoly. The Hudson's Bay achieved the status of structural monopoly when it merged with the North West Company in 1821.

The key to success is large scale, and the ability to achieve it and set the standard for effective competition through economies of scale, speed, etc. If you can set a large scale as a standard, so that the competition has to operate on a similarly large scale, you'll effectively limit that competition to those few who can muster that "minimal indivisible unit of investment." Needless to say, once these monopoly-scale structures and institutions are in place, they become powerful agents influencing future developments. Furthermore, they can usually count on the support, grudging or wholehearted, of everyone whose livelihood, and even way of life, depends on them.

The Hudson's Bay's systems and the agendas for development they embodied did, in fact, strongly influence the political destiny of Canada from the 1760s into the late 19th century. In fact, Innis' reading of key political developments, from the *Act of Union* to Confederation and even the National Policy, is that they were thinly disguised ruses for financing various transportation infrastructures from canals in the timber era to railways in the industrial era.

This state support was augmented by the biases associated with unused capacity that was built into the systems themselves. As the supply of furs began to diminish, merchants looked to something else to fill their ships' holds and discovered lumber for the London-bound crossing, and settler-immigrants to bring back.

"Governor George Simpson on a tour of Rupert's Land" by L.L. Fitzgerald (from a photo of a painting by Cyrus C. Cuneo)
Hudson's Bay Company Archives, Manitoba

This cyclical extension of staples-exporting systems is the core of Innis' and others' arguments that staples exports became a dominant pillar of Canadian development, with more local and diversified development subordinated to the priorities of staples. In a related argument, Canadian development was seen in an international context of Europe-centred trade and commerce.

There is no disputing that the infrastructures laid down over the long history of the fur trade left a permanent mark on the landscape of this country. The effects can be identified today in the large-scale systems associated with digital multi-media communications and their institutional agents. But it's important to challenge the inevitability of the patterns of development associated with these systems, patterns that have been highlighted by official texts and storytelling. If other patterns can be detected in other stories, they might also uncover other possibilities for designing and organizing communication in the present.

TURNING THE FRAME AROUND: THE FUR TRADE VIEWED FROM HERE In today's global information society, a critical awareness of material technologies and their power to shape politics, economics and culture is not enough. It's equally important to understand the technologies of knowledge and perception — technologies that shape our everyday sense of reality. Module III goes into this in great detail, with one unit devoted exclusively to how monopolies can develop in the area of knowledge and perception. Here, the intention is simply to introduce this theme, and to show how important it is to question conventional wisdom.

It can be argued that Harold Innis, like others writing about the fur trade, operated within the frame of conventional wisdom on "development."

"Fundamentally the civilization of North America is the civilization of Europe ...," Innis wrote in *The Fur Trade*. In *A History of the CPR*, he wrote that, "The history of the Canadian Pacific Railroad is primarily the history of the spread of western civilization over the northern half of the North American continent." By this, he primarily meant, European technique and technology, epitomized by merchant sailing ships, but also the technologies of rifles and York boats, and later, canals and railway lines. Although he mentions some native technologies, and even acknowledges how essential these were to the early days of the fur trade, his focus is on the more "advanced and specialized" technologies associated with European manufacturing. He ignores many of the native technologies as technologies, particularly the technologies produced and maintained by native women.

These gaps suggest that there's a whole other perspective to be gained, as well as important knowledge to be recovered, by turning the frame around and looking at the fur trade from here. Taking this other view, one realizes immediately that trading furs and other materials was part of a rich native economy that had flourished in North America long before the time of European contact.

Recent revisionist historical research and writing associated with Women's Studies and Native Studies illuminates this different perspective. Sylvia Van Kirk's *Many Tender Ties* (see box) is particularly useful in its detailed rethinking of the Canadian fur-trading story from the perspective of the native women involved. It points out that native women were integral to the fur trade and critical to its success. While Van Kirk doesn't address herself to native technology as such, her and others' writings are revealing.

There were material technologies, such as moccasins, canoes and snowshoes, that women primarily made. As

Apart from the assistance rendered by Indian women in general, Hudson's Bay Company travellers found it to their advantage to have their own particular "bedfellow" who could be most valuable in acquainting them with Indian custom. In 1692, when Henry Kelsey returned from the first inland voyage ever undertaken by a Hudson's Bay Company man, he was accompanied by a Cree woman whom he called his wife and insisted that she be allowed to enter the fort. Anthony Henday's "bedfellow" proved invaluable; besides preparing his "winter rigging", she provided him with crucial information about the designs of her countrymen. His woman enabled him to avoid a dangerous confrontation by advising him to stop pressing his party of Cree to hunt for furs because they intended to trade them with the Blackfoot in the spring. Henday protected his ally from the other Indians who might have killed her had they discovered her complicity, and when the scarcity of provisions reduced most of the women to subsist on berries, he felt obliged to give her a share of his meat.

In the decades prior to the establishment of the Company's first inland post In 1774, the men began to make frequent trips into the interior to counteract the devastating competition of the "Pedlars". The London Committee expressed concern that the men would "go native", but the early Hudson's Bay Company inlanders were unavoidably dependent upon the Indians, and it became customary for them to take a "canoe Mate & Tent Mate". "Women" declared one prominent inlander "are as useful as men upon journeys." Certainly many of the Company's important inland officers in the late eighteenth century — William Tomison, Robert Longmoor, Malchom Ross and William Walker — were greatly assisted in their successful adaptation to life in the interior by their Indian wives.

It was not unusual for an Indian woman to he found in the elevated role of guide owing to her availability and familiarity with the terrain. The elder Henry when going into the Churchill River area in 1776 employed an Indian woman as guide, remarking that she had served Mr. Frobisher in the capacity. The importance of the woman as guide is shown in the Nor'Westers' attempt to cripple Hudson's Bay

Company operations at Île à la Crosse in 1810 by intimidating the servant's wife who was guiding their brigade. An angry Peter Fidler recorded: "When our Men passed the Frog portage McTavish frightened our pilot away & it was two Days detention to them before they got her again — without her our men could not have come forward."

Because of her intimate contact with the traders, the Indian woman also played an important role as an interpreter and teacher of language. At least some understanding of the native languages was required to be an effective "indian trader", a fact readily grasped by the Nor'Westers. The less fluent Hudson's Bay Company men were assisted by Indian women in extending the trade. In 1753 John Potts at Richmond on the east side of Hudson's Bay avowed that his sole purpose in sending for a certain woman from Albany had been her perfect understanding of the Eastmain Indians, which differed very much from what he was used to. She rendered "Great Service to the company as an interpreter" and taught Potts the language so he could now make the Indians "Sensible" of his intentions. In the Brandon House area as late as 1819, the English still relied upon women to act as interpreters with the Assiniboine, whose language belonged to the Siouan linguistic group and not the more widespread Algonkian. Both companies used women as interpreters to communicate with tribes of the rich Lake Athabasca region. During his first winter at Fort Wedderburn, Simpson soon discovered one of the reasons for his rivals' strong position: the Nor'Westers' women were "faithful to their cause and good Interpreters whereas we have but one in the Fort that can talk Chipewyan". That one was the redoubtable Madame Lamallice, the wife of the Hudson's Bay Company brigade guide.

Simpson observed that Indian women could often serve as diplomatic agents for the traders. In hiring a French-Canadian to help extend the trade into the Great Slave Lake area, he was motivated by the fact that the man's wife was extensively connected among the Yellowknife and Chipewyan tribes there and would be able to overcome any prejudices "that our Opponents may have instilled in their minds against us."

Van Kirk, Sylvia, 1980. *Many Tender Ties: Women in Fur-Trade Society, 1670-1870.* Winnipeg: Watson & Dwyer.

well, there were the technologies of food preparation, such as making pemmican and turning corn into a host of edible foods. There were also the techniques and technologies used to prepare furs and cure hides, and to make clothes, tents and sleeping robes.

But perhaps the most important technologies, for the purposes of this course, were those of communication. Native women were important mediators in the fur-trading process. They served as translators and as negotiators between tribes involved in the fur trade. Finally, they engaged in the intimate communication of country marriages with the white traders. This cemented social bonds between the white and native communities and opened lines of negotiation between the local native society and economy and the European society and economy epitomized by the Hudson's Bay Company and its ways of doing business.

When you balance this view with the traditional view (the view from here with the view from there), you can see that the fur trade succeeded through a combination of communication: the long-distance commercial lines of communication associated with the Hudson's Bay Company and its merchant sailing ships, plus the local and more intimate lines of communication associated with face-to-face negotiations, personal conversation and even "pillow talk." While the former embodied what Innis called the dominant bias (of space) in modern communication, the latter embodied more of the bias associated with time — the non-material, more spiritual values associated with family, tradition and reciprocity within the tribe and community.

It's interesting to consider the implications of this different perspective on communication/transportation technologies in the fur trade, especially for public policy. The dominant thrust of communication/transportation policy in Canada has supported the space bias: fast, distance-spanning communication, usually requiring a lot of capital investment behind it. Perhaps a better balance between space-biased and time-biased communication, in policy and financial support, would have been fairer.

Technology doesn't emerge on its own, however. It's intimately bound up with concepts of "growth," "development" and other broad social goals and projects. The short-distance, local communication within communities where the fur trade was part of people's daily lives might have promoted development and growth as sustainable communities and family units. As we know, however, the commercial shipping and trading lines were given prominence, and they advanced development and growth in the form of market expansion and international trade. As this conception of growth and development was given priority in Canadian history, so also was a broader conception of social development, reflecting the priorities of both genders, all social classes and racial groups, relatively neglected by comparison.

"Mrs. James Rutherford, a native of the Red River Settlement, came to Moose Factory by canoe in the 1840s. She was a domestic in the household of Chief Factor Robert Miles and during her lifetime was a staunch and loyal Hudson's Bay Co. employee.

Her duties were many, ranging from the supervision of the large dairy to the nursing of the sick. During the fruit season, she supervised the making of all jams, jellies, etc. for the Officers' Mess, and at the annual slaughtering time, looked after the preparation of all meats, etc. A first-class seamstress and barberess, she was kept busy summer and winter.

In the social life of the Bay, she shone par excellence, a beautiful dancer and an expert demonstrator of the famous Red River jig.

She married James Rutherford, the company's blacksmith."

(Hudson's Bay Company Archives, Manitoba)

TURNING THE FRAME AROUND: SETTLER COMMUNITIES Douglas McCalla is one of several economic and social historians who have challenged the conventional wisdom that asserts the centrality of staples exports to Canadian development. He's done so by switching from the macro-scale of analysis associated with large-scale internationally framed development to a micro-scale more appropriate for seeing local development on its own terms. He's taken seriously all the small-scale enterprises from farms operating on a mixed subsistence and commercial basis to craft-scale local manufacturing and merchants. And he's concluded that they add up to considerable economic development. Taking seriously what Innis and others had largely ignored, he and others doing similar research have revised the historical record on what "development" in Canada has primarily been about.

Perhaps it hasn't been *primarily* about anything. Perhaps it's simply been that some people's projects were privileged over others, and treated as primary. But is that fair? And what are the policy implications of this? Is it just that the public should be burdened with debt for infrastructure projects supporting development conceived as primarily staples exports and trade in manufactured goods when this had little to do with the development experienced by many of the people who lived here: the settler population plus the native and Metis communities? A mixed policy approach might have been fairer and more appropriate: one supporting intensive local development through good local roads, footpaths and water routes as well as fast extensive transportation systems such as railways (see box).

> "The Canadian Pacific Railway, as a vital part of the technological equipment of western civilization, has increased to a very marked extent the productive capacity of that civilization. It is hypothetical to ask whether under other conditions, production would have been increased or whether such production would have contributed more to the welfare of humanity." (Innis, 1971:294)

This discussion of the fur trade from the perspective of Canada's first people reminds us that the bias of communication toward fast, global systems supported by large-scale capital investments is not a total or exclusive one. Still, it's important to realize how dominant that bias has always been.

As Harold Innis showed, the fur trade set the bias of space in communication to work in the northern half of North America. As money was invested in these transportation systems, and as they were extended outward across the country and forward into other forms of transportation, they helped install a particular model of development as well. This was large-scale commercial development particularly geared to international trade with the metropolitan centres of empires. All these developments have influenced the position of Canada today in the global economy and global cultural village.

This position has influenced Canada's unique discourse on technology, pioneered by the likes of Harold Innis and continued by George Grant, Marshall McLuhan and, more recently, Ursula Franklin. Others in this discourse, Irene Spry, Judith Stamp, Robert Babe, Vincent Mosco, Daniel Drache, Alison Beale, Margaret Benson and Lorna Roth, are included in the course, but these four thinkers will be featured primarily.

COMMENTARY ON SUPPLEMENTARY READINGS

1) Irene M. Spry, "Overhead Costs, Rigidities of Productive Capacity and the Price System."

The author makes the following points:

* The connection between overhead costs and flexible versus rigid systems. Essentially, if the minimal overhead capital investment required to participate in an activity is small — as in the fishery organized around individual ships — the system is flexible. If the minimum overhead cost is large — as happened with the intricately integrated trading and transportation system associated with the fur trade, the system becomes more rigid and unstable.

* High investment represented a high risk for investors; however, this was offset by rigidities in financing, such as the rigid requirement to make regular interest payments whether or not money was coming in. The risk was progressively passed along as, for instance, the owners of the transportation systems charged high fixed freight rates on canals and railways. It was the end users of these systems, the Prairie farmers for example, who were often left holding the bag when the market took a dive, bringing risk home to roost in the form of depressed resource markets.

* A cost becomes a rigid investment in productive capacity once money has been sunk into material systems and infrastructures required for production. Once cash is sunk into York boats, paddlewheelers and trading posts, or into bridges, canals and railway tracks, cost rigidities take it out of the realm of perfect competition into an imperfect world marked by efforts to control competition and through structural monopolies and rigid pricing structures.

* Those industries and institutions that operate as structural monopolies occupy a different sphere of the economy than smaller-scale independent operators. The evidence of economic history also shows that with their large-scale rigidities they can organize and plan to protect their interests, often to the detriment of others'.

* Equilibrium for the centre often means disequilibrium for the margins.

2) Harold Innis, "Transportation as a Factor in Canadian Economic History," from *Essays in Canadian Economic History*.

Note the following points:

* the connection between trans-Atlantic transportation and Canadian development, especially as the extraction of resources.

* the ongoing cycles of staples extraction from fish to fur to lumber, then to wheat, ores and pulp and paper, and so on.

* how geography, especially the waterways plus the terrain through which they travelled, and the strengths and weaknesses of different technologies of transportation shaped the pattern of development.

* how the rigidity of unused capacity in the return trip to Canada in the lumber era biased development in a new way toward settler immigration. Settlers solved the problem of unused capacity by providing revenue to ship owners on the crossing to Canada.

* the connection between staples-export development and development of large-scale space-bridging transportation and communication infrastructures such as canals and railways.

* the connection between political institutions and policies (notably fiscal policy) on the one hand and the need to finance large infrastructures on the other. Innis argues here that the *Act of Union* was largely a device whereby a larger political unit could lever more revenue (from tariffs which Finance Minister Alexander Galt also raised) for large-scale canal building. The idea was to extend the marketing reach of London-based manufacturers by removing cost barriers associated with privately funded transportation, thus helping to bring these goods within reach of the colonists. Later much the same philosophy was applied to extend the market reach of central Canadian manufacturers through the Inter-Colonial Railway.

* the tie-in between the National Policy (1879) and western railway building by the CPR. If the tariff on imported manufactured goods worked, it would guarantee a western market for eastern manufacturing interests using the railway to reach that market. If the tariff didn't block imports, the government could use the tariff revenues to cover its railway building costs.

* how transportation systems illustrate a point about monopoly scale and the smallest indivisible unit of investment, and why they have often been operated as state monopolies in the public interest. A canal system cannot start making money after only one lock is built, but only after the entire chain of locks is completed. Similarly a railway system requires a large indivisible initial investment in locomotives, cars, tracks and support services before the first train can leave the station.

SOURCES AND FURTHER READINGS

Innis, Harold, 1970. *The Fur Trade in Canada: An Introduction to Canadian Economic History*. Toronto: Ryerson.

Innis, Harold, 1956. *Essays in Canadian Economic History*, ed. Mary Q. Innis. Toronto: University of Toronto Press.

Innis, Harold, 1971. *A History of the Canadian Pacific Railway*. Toronto: University of Toronto Press.

McCalla, Douglas, 1993. *Planting the Province: The Economic History of Upper Canada, 1784-1870*. Toronto: University of Toronto Press.

Spry, Irene M., 1981. "Overhead Costs, Rigidities of Productive Capacity and the Price System," *Culture, Communication and Dependency: The Tradition of H.A. Innis*, eds. W. Melody, L. Salter and P. Heyer. Norwood, N.J.: Ablex Publishing

Van Kirk, Sylvia, 1991. *Many Tender Ties: Women in Fur-Trade Society, 1670-1870*. Winnipeg: Watson and Dwyer.

QUESTIONS FOR DISCUSSION

The following questions are meant to help you synthesize what you've learned here with what you know already. They'll help you test your comprehension of the key concepts discussed in this unit. They are also meant as a springboard into discussion sessions.

1) How is a phone call with a friend different from one to a 1-800 number? Is the telephone a tool in one instance and a system in another? What makes the difference?
2) Why is a railway system more rigid than a shipping line or a fleet of horse-drawn carriages?
3) What is an opportunity cost?
4) Name three things that contribute to "rigidities" in technological systems.
5) How did the Hudson's Bay Company's transportation/communication systems embody the bias of communication in the modern era? What is that bias and what does it mean?

CHAPTER 2

"UNPACKING THE BLACK BOX OF TECHNOLOGY"

OVERVIEW

This is the first of two units explaining how technology is at once a social construct reflecting certain choices and values, and at the same time a social force shaping subsequent choices through the values built into it. This unit looks at the nuts and bolts of technology as material, cultural and political-economic constructions. The third unit looks at the values and world view behind that social construct. Together, these units will attempt to bring home the main point of the course: the importance of taking technology into account in history, geography, economics, political economy, cultural studies and so on. It's equally important to understand the interplay of these factors in shaping technology and the unfolding post-industrial society.

This chapter in particular will also introduce some critical thinking tools, or concepts, for thinking about technology. These tools will be useful for the rest of the course.

We begin by challenging some of the conventional wisdom on how technology is perceived by the general public. We will then go through the various ways of thinking about technology as a social construct: as ***holistic tools***, versus ***prescriptive systems***; as expressing certain ***contingencies*** or choice paths; as incorporating ***systemic biases***. We will elaborate on concepts introduced in the first unit, such as ***rigidities*** in ***rigid productive systems***, and introduce the idea of technology operating at the non-material level of organized discussions and knowledge systems called ***discourse***. Finally we will put these concepts together to suggest not only that we live in a fully realized "technological" society, but why it is important critically to understand what this means.

OBJECTIVES

When you have completed this unit, you should be able to answer the following questions:

1) How is a computer both a tool and part of a huge system? How is a car both a tool and part of a huge system?
2) Why is contingency important in understanding the idea of choice in technology? How is contingency linked to time?
3) How does systemic bias operate through technological systems? How does it make technology appear to be deterministic?

THE VIDEO BEGINS by revisiting the themes explored in Unit 1: the connection between the bias of fast, space-bridging communication technology and global market development, and how this was depicted as the epitome of human progress in the modern era. But was it progress for everyone, and as everyone would define it? The question opens the prospect of other choice paths, other story lines and the struggle between differing values and priorities associated with different groups and institutions in society.

Much of that choice, and that struggle, is hidden behind the seemingly value-neutral surface of technology: everything from railway systems and expressway overpasses to computers and television sets. To get at those choices, to reveal the biases built into virtually every technological system, you have to open the black box of technology. You have to "deconstruct" technology to reveal it as the social construct it is.

THREE WAYS OF THINKING ABOUT TECHNOLOGY Ask yourself, what comes to mind when you think of technology? Make a list of whatever first pops into your head. Ask a friend, or other members of your family. Almost invariably, students first mention the latest in high-technology gadgets first: computers, cell phones, plus television, fax, phone and the Internet. Can you detect a bias here? Obviously, there's a bias toward "the latest" technology over traditional time-tested technologies. There's also a bias toward something called "high" technology over an implied "low" technology, which is usually less complex and less expensive.

Heather Menzies at the National Museum of Science and Technology, Ottawa

But there are other biases, buried even more deeply than this. One is a bias toward technology as a concrete thing, a commodity. There's a related bias toward technologies used by individuals, and often as consumers rather than workers. But what about the technological infrastructures that support our lives in almost every conceivable way: everything from air-conditioning systems and elevators to traffic-management systems, management information systems running libraries and universities, power and utility systems? These technologies seem the least present, the most invisible of all.

This isn't surprising, considering how technology is most commonly represented in our society. It's depicted as a tool that the individual end user can control as he or she sees fit. This is a liberal view of technology, assuming individual autonomy and control. The assumption is that the technology itself is neutral, and can be used for good or for ill depending on the values of the individual user. Consumer technologies, and computers and faxes operated by business professionals, best approximate this conception of technology. Even here, however, the autonomy is often limited, by the infrastructure, for instance, and individual choice is often restricted to multiple choice (see ***discourse*** later in this unit).

The second popular view of technology is almost the flip side of the first. This is the deterministic view. A fairly conservative perspective, it sees technology as a deterministic force over which individuals have little or no control. This view tends to prevail in cases of large-scale technology and technological change, such as global economic restructuring. Globalization is discussed in the popular media as though it's a hurricane or other force of nature: something to which nations and people have to adjust themselves, on the terms provided.

This course introduces a third way of looking at technology: as a social and historical construction. This view sees technology as a tool for some people and a deterministic system for others, depending on the social relations involved, for example. This third perspective examines the connections between tools and larger-scale systems by looking at how material artifacts are combined in social organizations, with certain social relations imposed or negotiated within them.

TECHNOLOGY: *TECHNE/LOGOS*

From the Greek words *techne* for art or craft, and *logos* for word.

"The application of science, especially to industrial or commercial objectives." *The American Heritage Dictionary*

"A discourse or treatise on an art or the arts; the scientific study of the practical or industrial arts." *The Oxford English Dictionary*

Take the car as an example. On the one hand, it is a tool, even a tool of personal liberation, given the tone of the typical automobile ad on television. Once you're behind the wheel, you can go anywhere at any time. You're free to move! But at the same time, you are constrained by the various systems of which you become a part once you buy and start driving the car: the urban expressway system with its limited exits and entry points and its built-in trade-off of mass-motorist speed for personal flexibility. There's also the insurance and highway regulatory system, plus the financing system associated with buying and maintaining the car in the first place.

This suggests that you can understand a lot more about technology when you stop thinking about a particular technology in isolation, and start thinking about it in the context of technological practice.

TECHNOLOGY AS PRACTICE Ursula Franklin takes this grounded view of technology, defining technology, after Kenneth Boulding, as how we do things around here. This inclusive approach shifts the focus from artifacts (tools) to the social processes and social relations associated with getting things done. It's an inclusive approach to technology, taking in everything from the know-how of knitting and making crabapple jelly to the technologies of prayer and organizational bureaucracy. Being inclusive, it acknowledges all the skill and knowledge people bring to developing technique and applying technology. This view includes women who are often depicted as being "outside technology" because definitions of technology usually eclipse women's technological practice, such as baking, cooking, nursing babies, fixing the washing machine or xerox machine (see box: dictionary definitions). Often this is experience-based knowledge, called tacit knowledge. It is informal knowledge passed on from mother to daughter, neighbour to friend. It's not the formal credentialed knowledge associated with designing and operating the "high" technology of industry. But it's real knowledge nonetheless, and vital to getting things done in the economy of everyday life.

Looking at technology as social practice also allows us to fill what is often a gap of perception between tool and system, for it allows us to see tools as flowing out of and being part of organized social processes or systems. This perspective then lets us ask what kind of system it is: whether it's open and democratic or closed and, to some degree or other, authoritarian; not just a system of production, or communication, but also a system of control.

One way of distinguishing here is between holistic and prescriptive technologies (see box). This distinction, which views the artifacts of tool and system within the dynamic context of social action, also helps us to identify the social components of technology. These include social relations, knowledge and how it's controlled, plus various structures of social organization, such as specialized division of labour. It also allows us to see that technology involves capital investments and takes shape (sometimes rigid shape) over time.

HOLISTIC/PRESCRIPTIVE TECHNOLOGIES

Holistic technologies and technological practice centre control of the technology in the hands (and head) of the user, the doer, the technological practitioner. In this form of technological practice, which can best be compared to craft production, the individual controls the technology and the work to be done from the conceptual, creative phase to the practical completion of it. The technological practice can be spontaneous and infinitely varied.

With prescriptive technologies and technological practice, however, the conception and control of work are separated from the doing of the work. The work is set down as a series of fragmented tasks and prescribed actions in a specialized division of labour, which is controlled externally.

TECHNOLOGY IN TIME AND SPACE The notion of *contingency*, or technological choice paths, widens our understanding of technology from social construct to historical construct as well. Technologies will often develop along a fairly distinct time line. There's an initial innovation and invention phase, where the technology is often used holistically and applied in a variety of playful as well as useful ways. This is followed by a growth phase, or what one of my 1996-97 students, John MacNab, calls an "enterprise" stage, where certain uses of the technology become institutionalized and systems grow up to support them. But there's still a lot of contingency, or choice, and usually still a lot of scope for holistic technological practice. However, this phase is often followed by a corporate consolidation phase, in which uses of the technology become increasingly prescribed by technological systems. The systems themselves are consolidated and become increasingly rigid, and alternative uses, or contingencies, are marginalized or shut down completely.

Ursula Franklin, Professor Emerita, University of Toronto. Gerald Turner

In studying the history of particular technologies and technological practices, we can sometimes identify critical moments where one choice path was consolidated and another marginalized, and where one value or priority took precedence over others. The history of telephone use is illustrative here. In the early 1900s, a device that users could install in their telephone boxes to protect their privacy on multi-user lines opened a path for greater user control of the phone. With this device, users could have arranged their own conference calls and even used the phone for quasi broadcasting, while avoiding the expense of private lines (Martin, 1991:21). However, this development path was cut off as the telephone companies directed developments toward a centrally controlled system in which they controlled all the switching along individualized single-user lines. It was by far the more expensive development choice; but it delivered on the values of centralized control and restrictive end-user participation.

Still, there was considerable scope for local control through locally operated switchboards. Often the sole representative of the telephone company in a community, local switchboard operators had a fairly free hand in putting the new technology to use. As Ursula Franklin has noted, they were largely responsible for its development as a domestic tool of communication and as a medium of community culture. Much as community freenet and list-serve operators are creating community networking services through the Internet today, early switchboard operators created an all-purpose community-information service as they patched people through to doctors' offices and the firehall, gave out the time and even broadcast community announcements. In fact, it was the operators' knowledge and expertise as communicators that compensated for the technical unreliability of the early telephones and prompted people to subscribe to the service (Martin, 1991:98). However, as the system reached the corporate consolidation phase, operators were more and more restricted to fragmented prescriptive job functions which have become increasingly automated. Furthermore, the development path of communications as local culture and community was all but eclipsed as the corporate infrastructures asserted a more strictly commercial model, of communications as transactions (see Units 7, 8 and 10 for more on this theme).

Once technology has been developed into a rigid system that can be controlled as a whole from a remote centre, this kind of technology can then bias or influence other technological choice and development paths. The triumph of the electric fridge over the quieter and more economical gas-powered model is a fascinating case in point. One company in particular, General Electric, was crucial in shifting the development of fridges from a gas-powered model to an electric one. It achieved this in the 1920s through a massive advertising and promotional campaign enlisting the support of high-profile clients of industrial electricity, such as Henry Ford. By comparison, the manufacturers of gas-absorption fridges "lacked the large sums of money, the armies of skilled personnel, the competitive pressure and the aggressive assistance of utility companies" that the electric-fridge makers like G.E. had at their disposal (Schwartz Cowan, 1985:211). They lacked the scale of a commercial infrastructure.

> "Edison invented systems.... After conceiving in general and sweeping terms of a system of incandescent lighting in the fall of 1878, Edison announced his brainchild with fanfare in the *New York Sun* on October 20, 1878. Always good newspaper copy, he told reporters of plans for underground distribution in mains from centrally located generators in the great cities; predicted that his electric light would be brought into private houses and simply substituted for the gas burners at a lower cost; and confidently asserted that his central station would furnish 'light to all houses within a circle of half a mile.' He spoke not only of his incandescent lamp but of other envisaged components of his system, such as meters, dynamos, and distribution mains." (Hughes, 1985:39)

The most obvious and pervasive bias built into large-scale systems is the industrial, commercial bias.

As Unit 1 made clear, the bias of space is advanced through market expansionism using various media, or methods, of space-spanning transmission and distribution. As that unit also made clear, this bias has shaped the dominant political, economic and cultural institutions of this country, gearing them materially toward commercial development and politically toward centralized control over people and places (regions). The effect has also been reciprocal. Development favours the continuing promotion of technologies that encourage market expansion, which has contributed significantly to the dominance of global digital communication technologies today.

There are a range of other biases contributing to what Langdon Winner has called "technological politics," including biases favouring the privileged and able-bodied. There are sexist biases in the organization of work, and its lack of flexibility to accommodate childbearing, child rearing and other family-related priorities. There are similar biases in the construction of facilities without women's washrooms, change rooms or showers.

The story of Robert Moses and the construction of overpasses for the Long Island freeway shows how bias operates through the seemingly neutral guise of technology, and how racism can be built into technological systems. American civil engineer, Robert Moses, built his racism into the construction of overpasses on the New York freeway out to Jones' Beach on Long Island by designing them so low that the city buses, carrying less privileged African-Americans from Harlem, couldn't get through. According to Moses' biographer, this wasn't accidental. It was part of Moses' design (Winner, 1985:28).

"The things we call 'technologies' are ways of building order in our world.... In that sense technological innovations are similar to legislative acts or political foundings that establish a framework for public order that will endure for many generations." (Winner, 1985:30)

The typewriter is a significant case study as it shows how a seemingly isolated tool (the typewriter) is tied into a series of systems large enough to be called infrastructure, and also how an initial bias was built into it from the beginning. Christopher Sholes' QWERTY keyboard design earned him the title of "father of the typewriter" not because it particularly helped typists, but because it prevented keys from jamming in the carriage. It put machine efficiency over human efficiency. A later design, the Dvorak design, was shown to improve typists' speed and reduce typing errors. But by then, as Elaine Bernard points out, an infrastructure of factories tooled to make the Sholes model, typing schools dedicated to teaching it and millions of typists trained on that keyboard prevented the other choice path from flourishing (Bernard, 1984:13).

This example highlights the importance of infrastructure, the sometimes forgotten backdrop to technological tools. Infrastructures can not only limit the choices of how tools can be used, for instance, through pricing policies and availability. They can often determine what tools will become available in the first place. They can restrict freedom of choice to multiple choices, with the choices themselves defined by others.

PLANNING, DISCOURSE AND COMPLIANCE So far, I've described technology largely from the material viewpoint of structures and social relations. But it should also be understood through its immaterial or non-material components: the cultural elements of planning, discourse and cultural compliance.

Planning is the partner of prescriptive technology, a critical feature in the development of large-scale technological infrastructures and the site where government and industry negotiate the meaning and priorities of development. At its most fundamental, prescriptive technology hinges on a separation of the conception of work from its actual performance. Division of labour and organizations of work achieve this separation in space. Planning achieves it in time. Prescriptive technology turns the planners' present into the plannees' future, and turns what is known and decided by the planner into what is not yet known by the people on the receiving end. The technology is thereby placed outside the realm of these people's control and decision making. Through planning, the future potential for of action is transformed into a set of prescribed actions, or a multiple choice among a pre-determined set of alternatives. What might have been open for negotiation among the participants in a particular situation is closed and restricted through advance planning. Certain contingencies are excluded from the design options, from the protocols, and from the sense of what's possible and desirable.

> "In political terms, prescriptive technological systems are designs for compliance." (Franklin, 1990:23)

This, in Ursula Franklin's view, is one of the key roles of planning. It is a technology that can channel public discussion and perception of "what is doable, and what is not." This is done through various channels or media generally associated with public discourse, including government committees and the media that report on them, academic and other "experts" and the publications that give them credibility by publishing their statements as official and formal knowledge. (The social construction of knowledge, particularly as official public knowledge, is discussed more fully in Unit 9.)

Discourse can be understood as a cultural technology. It's an organized system of discussion which, like any system, can be open or closed, depending on the rules and the structures adopted. It doesn't exclude or silence discussion through an outright conspiracy of exclusion. It merely contains and guides it through its frames and terms of reference. Like the overpasses on Robert Moses' expressway, the systems include or exclude through a built-in or systemic bias, not a rudely overt one. By and large, the biases expressed through the terms and frame of reference reflect the biases prevailing in the technological landscape they're discussing. One of the most prominent is the tendency of discourses dealing with technology (everything from women's infertility and new reproductive technologies to digital technologies and the post-industrial workplace) to focus on technology, not on the larger context, and the priorities of the people and places within it.

The discourse surrounding the adoption of the gasoline tractor on Western Canadian farms in the 1940s is instructive. One account (Ankli *et al.*, 1980:9-31) begins by critiquing the prevailing tendency to focus on farm machinery rather than on farmers' priorities in their choice and use of technology. The authors marshall evidence to suggest that farmers in fact engaged in a vigorous debate about the pros and cons of capital-intensive mechanization; they didn't just adopt the technology simply because it was there. For example, farmers weighed their existing competence and capacity to fix simple horse-drawn implements against the costly dependence associated with machines someone else would have to fix, and initially refused the tractor option. They changed their minds, however, when the government-controlled Canadian Wheat Board implemented a policy biasing farming toward extensive acreage. It then made economic sense to switch from real horse power to mechanized horse power.

> "**B**ut when technique enters into every area of life, including the human, it ceases to be external to man and becomes his very substance. It is no longer face to face with man but is integrated with him, and it progressively absorbs him.... Completely natural and spontaneous effort is replaced by a complex of acts designed to improve, say, the yield." (Ellul, 1969:6,20)

Despite the critical strength of the essay, it has one major flaw. There is never any suggestion of a larger frame of reference: that farming may involve priorities other than market economic ones; nor any reference to priorities about long-term survival of the family or long-term sustainability of the land. There was no suggestion of valuing the pace of life associated with "horse time," and valuing the option of working with living creatures rather than machines.

These omissions point to the topic in the next unit: the role of mind set and world view informing our sense of reality and our sense of what is relevant vis à vis technology and life generally.

This mind set is like a second skin, so close to us and comfortingly familiar that we hardly notice how its assumptions work on us, influencing what technologies we choose over others, and our predisposition to think in certain ways about technology.

> "[**O**]ur activities of knowing and making have been brought together in a way that does not allow the once-clear distinguishing of them. In fact, the coining of the word technology catches the novelty of that co-penetration of knowing and making. It also implies that we have brought the sciences and the arts into a new unity in our will to be masters of the earth and beyond....
>
> We close down on the fact that modern technology is not simply an extension of human making through the power of a perfected science but is a new account of what it is to know and to make in which both activities are changed by their co-penetration."(Grant, 1986:11)

This is what Conservative philosopher, George Grant, grappled with in his critiques of technology in modern technological society. Building on the work of French sociologist Jacques Ellul (see box), he sensed that the modern era had fused the previously separate pursuits of know-how (technique) and of know-why (knowledge, philosophy) to create a new philosophy or way of being (ontology) which he called the will to technique, or mastery through technique. It is a philosophy and world view in which the pursuit of technical goals such as speed and productivity were taken as moral goals.

QUESTIONS FOR DISCUSSION

Again, the questions here are intended to stimulate a discussion in which you integrate the new concepts and ideas you've learned with the knowledge and ideas you already have. You could begin with the questions posed at the beginning of this chapter. Then, to test your knowledge a bit more, consider the following two questions:

1) What aspects of university learning are prescriptive and what aspects could be described as holistic? Why?
2) Do you think that the open choice paths associated with the Internet in its current "new technology" stage will continue over time?

COMMENTARY ON SUPPLEMENTARY READINGS

Ursula Franklin, *The Real World of Technology.*

There is lot of overlap between the points raised in the video and those raised in the readings. However, it's worth reviewing the assigned chapters for this unit (Chapters 1, 2 and 4) to ensure you understand the key insights they provide.

Chapter 1 introduces technology as a social/cultural construction enveloping us all.

* The image of "the house that technology built" addresses one of the recurring themes of this course: that technology is more than the sum of the machines that populate our daily lives. It's become the environment in which we live and work, an environment that increasingly encloses us and determines where we can go and what we can do.

* technology as an agent of power and control. Franklin sees technology in broadly cultural and even political terms, and as organized systems. But not all these systems are geared to power and control. Her example of knitting technique, viewed through her inclusive focus on technology as "practice," reminds us that technique and technology touch all aspects of life, and can be freely shared with friends.

* Dr. Franklin's research into the history of ancient Chinese bronze casting taught her the significance of prescriptive techniques as methods of social organization involving, as she puts it, "discipline and planning, organization and command." Through this, she also sees the emergence of the "production model" over the "growth model" as a prime organizational model in society. Thus in education, the focus has shifted from personal growth to producing skill sets — products. As well, while growth is spontaneous yet governed by natural limits, production is planned and predictable and recognizes no limits to growth.

* Related to this, she points out that while there is a sophisticated science for counting people and populations, there is no machine demographics.

Chapter 2 makes a number of important points about the construction of public perception, through the structuring and control of discourse.

* Franklin differentiates between four versions of reality:

1) "vernacular reality," which is direct personal experience and how we directly perceive the world;
2) "extended reality," which is indirect experience, related by others or experienced indirectly through artifacts and other historical remains;

3) "constructed or reconstructed reality," which is brought to us by the mass media. This type of reality, she argues, sets up fundamental patterns of association in our minds, the mental maps we use in interpreting the details of daily life and figuring out what's important;
4) "projected reality," which is a blend of the others into an imagined future.

* Concentrating on constructed reality, she argues that the scientific method, which separates knowledge from experience by abstracting and objectifying it, is a critical technology, or set of methods. It produces a kind of production-model approach to constructing public perception. In fact, she argues, this model has become *the* model for defining reality rather than just one among many.

* This method not only glorifies expertise; it downgrades experience and silences vernacular reality and the insights it can provide in evaluating technology.

* The transmission of constructed reality, through high-speed communication, also influences what we perceive, and what is muted. Essentially, she argues that it brings news of far-away places into local neighbourhoods. But at the same time, these images and stories displace or marginalize what's really happening on the streets where we live.

* The mass media, with their constructed reality of "the far out-performing the near" and eclipsing personal and locally shared perceptions, for Franklin represent "an occupation force of immense power."

* They also impose unequal relations of communication. The technology, in its design, eliminates the chance of reciprocity, of people talking back, and actually changing the constructed reality of conventional wisdom as a result.

* She notes that reciprocity is responding on your own terms, while feedback is response on the terms provided.

* These systems for communicating constructed reality consign people to a state of "technologically-induced human isolation." Whereas, the reciprocal relations of ham radio operators allow people to be in touch with each other, and share their vernacular reality.

Chapter 4 concentrates on infrastructures and the importance of planning, particularly by government in support of industry, around these. The following points are important.

* Infrastructures have been important for the expansion of new technologies since the Industrial Revolution, and have been the main sites for government involvement in support of industrial development.

* There has been a consistently anti-people, anti-democratic bias in the design of these infrastructures. People (e.g. as organized labour) are often depicted as the problem; technology is the solution.

* Related to this bias, publicly funded infrastructures have consistently supported preparations for war. In fact, arms production has provided a convenient excuse for public funding of an infrastructure to support the advancement of technology. However, this requires a "credible long-term enemy." If not a foreign enemy, then an "enemy within."

* Part of that infrastructure is a bureaucracy for long-term planning, which helps to perpetuate the biases (including an assumption of enemies) in the technological infrastructures, and create self-fulfilling prophecies. Planning does this mostly by what it prevents, what it frames out of the planning discussion.

* Taxation is the financial means of supporting this infrastructure. It also means that citizens are involuntarily conscripted into supporting this generic war-readiness system.

* Planning is a tool of prescriptive technology and of a production-model approach to doing. It assumes the validity of pre-determined goals and objectives, the realization of which should take precedence over any present particulars of person or place.

* This dogmatic conformity to prescribed plans is in contrast to the experience she had as a first-time mother. The realities of a new-born child defied pre-planning. She learned to cope in the present rather than to plan for the future.

* The Berger Inquiry (into the Mackenzie Valley Pipeline) offers an alternative planning model, based more on the living context of the Mackenzie Valley rather than an abstract production plan (see Unit 9 for more detail on this).

* The production-model approach to planning leaves the living world out. But we are part of nature, and nature is powerful and alive.

* Part of any rethinking of our society as "the real world of technology" must involve focusing on context, and the experience of real people.

SOURCES AND FURTHER READINGS

Ankli, R.E., Helsberg, H.D. and Thompson, J.H., 1980. "The Adoption of the Gasoline Tractor in Western Canada," in *Canadian Papers in Rural History.* Vol. 2, ed. Donald H. Akenson. Ganonoque: Langdale Press.

Bernard, Elaine, 1984. "Science, Technology and Progress: Lessons from the History of the Typewriter," *Canadian Woman Studies/les cahiers de la femme,* 5(4).

Ellul, Jacques, 1964. *The Technological Society.* New York: Random House.

Franklin, Ursula, 1990. *The Real World of Technology.* Toronto: Anansi Press.

Grant, George, 1986. "The Morals of Modern Technology," *The Canadian Forum* (October).

Hughes, Thomas P., 1985. "Edison and Electric Light," in *The Social Shaping of Technology.* Donald MacKenzie and Judy Wajcman, eds. Milton Keynes: Open University Press.

Martin, Michele, 1991. *"Hello Central?" Gender, Technology and Culture in the Formation of Telephone Systems.* Montreal: McGill-Queens Press.

Mumford, Lewis, 1967. *The Myth of the Machine.* 2 Vols. New York: Harcourt Brace Jovanovich.

Schwartz Cowan, Ruth, 1985. "How the Refrigerator got its Hum," in *The Social Shaping of Technology.* D. MacKenzie and J. Wajcman, eds. Milton Keynes: Open University Press.

Winner, Langdon, 1985. "Do Artifacts have Politics?," in *The Social Shaping of Technology.* D. MacKenzie and J. Wajcman, eds. Milton Keynes: Open University Press.

CHAPTER THREE

"THE MIND, THE MACHINE AND THE LIVING EARTH"

OVERVIEW

The first unit introduced you to the idea that technology is more than the pen in your hand and the telephone at your elbow. It's also a set of systems and infrastructures that can fundamentally shape a society and determine who gets to use pens and telephones, for what purpose. The second unit picked apart technology as both a social construct and as a shaping force in its own right. It listed the various components of technology and technological practice: from materials in systems to social relations and bureaucratic rules and, finally, to the assumptions in the discourse that support it.

This unit looks more deeply into those assumptions and the world view they're part of. It will explore the dominant ways of knowing the world which have influenced the basic concept of technology in the modern era. In particular, it will focus on our ways of knowing the world materially: that is, through modern science (the word "science" comes from the Latin *sciere*, "to know").

It's hard to identify the assumptions associated with modern science and science-based technology from inside the society that has produced them, and is produced by them. It's like trying to distinguish the forest from the trees. To help do this, to see modern science and science-based technology as the social and cultural construct it is, we'll begin by looking at another culture's approach to science and technology: that of the First People of this country, and other parts of the world.

The video begins with a unique glimpse into a community where that way of knowing still flourishes. In an effort to represent native approaches to science and technology on their own terms, I interviewed three generations of Algonquin Indian elders, living in the bush outside the Rapid Lake Reserve in Northern Quebec. The commentary here will help you grasp the often subtle lessons revealed in this visit, drawing on native writing from outside as well as inside Canada.

The second part of this unit reviews the major philosophical traditions associated with "Western," or European, science and science-based technology. It introduces you to a range of elements, from the spirituality of Protestantism to the materialism of modern applied science, capitalism and utilitarianism, and the aesthetics of linear perspective. These underpin the mental maps that shape our sense of reality, including what constitutes "development."

The final section highlights the importance of these mental maps in the development of 19th-century Canada, and their continuing importance in shaping a sense of people's options in post-modern or late-modern society today.

OBJECTIVES The subject of this unit can easily fill a course and even a lifetime of study. However, this very brief introduction to native and western ways of knowing and doing (science and technology) is adequate for this course. The main idea is to make you critically aware of two things: 1) behind that initial listing of what technology is at the beginning of Unit 2 are the values and biases associated with modern science and modern liberal philosophy; 2) these are cultural constructs, and they can be challenged and changed. In other words, bridges can be built between, for example, native ways of knowing and the dominant ways of knowing associated with science-based technology. This can stimulate a rethinking of current approaches, perhaps along lines more conducive to a sustainable ecological society.

At the end of this unit, you should be able to answer the following questions:

1) How did modern science and modern liberal philosophy provide mental maps to support the fur trade?
2) What is the connection between modern science and prescriptive technologies?
3) How is the native approach to technology different from the modern European-based approach?

MUCH OF THE FIRST HALF of the video consists of conversations with three generations of Algonquin Indian elders living in log cabins in the bush outside the Rapid Lake Reserve in Northern Quebec. They are Jacob Wawatie, his mother, Irene Jerome, and her mother, Lena Nottaway, known as *Kokom*, or grandmother. After an initial weekend visit there in the company of a native colleague, Madelaine Dion Stout, a Cree Indian from Alberta who directs the Aboriginal Studies Centre at Carleton University, I returned with a video crew, and we spent a day together. I've tried to present the taped record of that visit in the same spirit, as a visit you're invited to join. As you'll notice, this segment is more "holistic" than "prescriptive" in the knowledge it imparts. It's knowledge imparted by stories and by showing; pointing out the ways of nature's knowledge.

Irene Jerome, Algonquin elder, Kokomville, Quebec

I encourage you to look at this portion of the video more than once, because the points being made are subtle and buried in the texture of the story. As you're watching, try to sense some of the principles at work in the native ways of knowing and doing, or science and technology, and how these differ from Western science and philosophy.

PRINCIPLES OF NATIVE SCIENCE This section title is somewhat misleading as native people writing about native science constantly stress that there is no one or "essential" native science. Each tribe or nation follows its own ways of knowing which are, as Pam Colorado puts it, specific to a locale. However, there are several common themes.

Perhaps the first common theme of native science is that people are part of nature, not apart from it. Related to this is the idea that nature is not static, not just inert material. It is alive and breathing. This life-giving breath unites all living things, including people, in nature's web of life, and it is sacred.

Two other principles of native science follow from this: first, that there's no distinction between the material level of the world and the spiritual level (the word "spirit" comes from the Latin verb *spirare*, "to breath"). In other words, the "shamanistic" traditions are grounded in the material practice of native science and technology. (In the video, this is suggested in what Jacob Wawatie says at the beginning about the drum representing the heartbeat of the living world, and later in what he says about making snowshoes and preparing to hunt.) The second principle of native science, which flows from the integral nature of its world view, is that everything is related to everything else. In fact, this is one of what Pam Colorado describes as the four "dynamics" at work in native science. These are:

1) feelings: "The nature of native science is that it is qualitative and subjective rather than quantitative and objective."
2) the historical "now": "Past present, future perfect and future exist at this moment." It's important to be attuned to that continuous dynamic, in the present.
3) prayer as a medicine: The metaphor for this is *Gii Laii*, the quiet still place of balance within ourselves. "It is an actual place and state of being that marks the endpoint/beginning of our science."
4) relations: "The Indian theory of relatedness demands that each and every entity in the universe seeks and sustains personal relationships."

> "Seeking truth and coming to knowledge necessitates studying the cycles, relationships and connections between things. Indeed a law of Native science requires that we look ahead seven generations when making decisions." (Colorado, 1988:51)

In Australia, philosopher of science Helen Verran has learned that relationships are at the heart of what she calls the Yolgnu Aboriginal "knowledge system." While Western science takes things apart and disembodies them from the larger whole, this Australian Aboriginal science studies them in their whole complexity. This doesn't make their science any less rigorous. In fact, Verran argues that it's just as rigorous, just as logical. But while Western scientific logic is based on numbers (isolated digital units), the logic at work in the clan society she's explored in Australia is based on kinship. Called *gurrutu*, it's a kinship system that takes family kinship as merely the starting point of a whole network of relationships that include plants and animals, land and water. People are named in relation to place, and place is part of a person's own particular map of identity. Related to this, people are responsible for knowledge specific to the land, water, animals, etc. of the place from which they come.

> "The *gurrutu* mesh," says Verran, "is like a very complex locating system," a sort of map of the world. But whereas with Western science we have to make our maps *a posteriori*, for the Yolgnu "the world comes to life already mapped." Their map is embedded in the very being of the world, and is quite inseparable from it. (Wertheim, 1995:40)

This dovetails with the importance of totems in Australian Aboriginal culture. Meaning flesh and soul combined in several Aboriginal languages, the totem represents a person's place in the world, in time. There are two ideas here: one is that the totemic ancestors were the original creators, and so to know the totemic links and be in harmony with them is to share an account of eternity and continuity from past to present and future. The second idea is that the soul is eternal, is in everything and moves not only from one human to another and from one generation to another, but from one living thing to another, and between the natural and supernatural worlds.

Another principle at work in native knowing and doing is that human beings aren't at the top of a pecking order of creation, but the youngest family members within it. As Vine Deloria, a Standing Rock Sioux who teaches at the University of Arizona explains, this has profound consequences: "as the youngest members of the living families, we were given the ability to do many things but not specific wisdom about the world. So our job was to learn from other older beings and to pattern ourselves after their behaviour." (Deloria, 1990:14)

"[W]hat gave creation its order and cohesion was the ability of souls to change flesh, to move from one bearer to another. Over time, a soul might move from a person to an animal to a star and back again. The group of things through which a soul could move formed a totem. People were thus related not so much to other people but to their totem, that is, that group of things in the natural and supernatural world through which their souls could move." (Gammage, 1992:6)

This posture is reflected in the traditions associated with learning native science and becoming a practitioner of native science and technology. One learns from the older ones, the elders, which includes animals and plants as well as older people. Pam Colorado explains that the tree is a respected elder because, "To the Indian, the tree is the first person on earth. Indeed, the tree which oxygenated earth's atmosphere, is the precursor to our human existence." (Colorado, 1988:50)

THE APPRENTICE AND NATIVE SCIENCE The centrality of relationships between living things united in a sacred webwork of life is reflected in native teaching/learning traditions. The core of this learning, of this knowledge system, is not the textbook or a laboratory. It's a relationship of a generally younger apprentice to an elder. It's not a professional relationship in the sense of working in a specialized institution. It's a highly personal and involved relationship, based on personal caring and respect.

Notice how much of this is reflected in the video. Jacob Wawatie refers to the "teachings" of his forefathers being worked into the snowshoes he makes. He also conveys his

"One of the tenets of American Indian science is that the search for truth and learning is a spiritual relationship between the individual and the Creator. The rule that governs the behaviour between elders and the younger learner is therefore that of helper rather than instructor....

The visit is an essential ingredient of native scientific methodology. The visit includes introductions, establishing the relationship between the elder and the younger person.... Through visits, a contract is established. Often the contracting process requires several visits, the apprentice will do chores around the elder's home, listen attentively and follow directions through mundane activities. Through this process, trust is established and a genuine interest in the welfare of the Elder is promoted. This is important — the Elder is about to share knowledge that is powerful, sacral and often of a personal nature. The recipient must be prepared.

In addition, the process of the visit teaches the younger person the qualities that are necessary for becoming a Native American scientist. These qualities include tremendous self-discipline, patience, a willingness to share, faith and a belief in prayer." (Colorado, 1988:56-57)

respect for their origin in the cycle of life as he hangs up his worn-out snowshoes in a tree in the sugar bush, giving them back with thanks. It's hardly throwing them away in the Western sense of the word.

Similarly, Irene Jerome, talking about the different medicines in the plants growing around the family's cabins in the bush, explains that she learned not only from her mother but from the animals. The same respect and humility comes through in the conversation with *Kokom*, Lena Nottaway, at the end of this segment as she talks about having learned the native ways of knowing and doing from her foremothers and forefathers. She refers to this knowledge and tradition — how to survive in the bush through her living relationships with the animals and plants growing there — as her "baggage" and her identity.

It is remarkable how immaterial that baggage is, an idea that is taken up in the Robin Riddington reading. The various technologies these people talked about — Jacob's snowshoes and preparations for a moose hunt, and Irene's herbal medicines — don't loom large as complex or expensive technologies in the Western sense of the word. They are rather an application of other elders' teachings, and of their own learned sense of being attuned to their environment. The spiritual aspect of this connectedness is suggested by the prayer-like ritual Jacob goes through in sharpening his knife. It is an action that illustrates his respect for the moose and the need to bring its cycle of life to a state of completion so it can give its body to the hunter. It's also suggested in Lena Nottaway's assertion that if she didn't have this knowledge, "I would be lost in my own culture, my own tradition."

Their technology is not only an extension of themselves; the drum a spiritual extension of the heart, the snowshoes an extension of the feet. It's an extension of a complex and interdependent living body of knowledge that sustains them and is sustained by them. It might be immaterial, but it can be destroyed just as fully as material structures can be.

You get a sense of this in Lena Nottaway's reflections. She not only talks about the destruction of the Indian people through the loss of their knowledge of living off the land and with the land. She also talks about the destruction of the land itself, through clear cutting in the region where she lives and by putting a monetary value on land in the first place.

She talks about how native people themselves are contributing to this dying by not keeping their knowledge alive through using it. Knowledge, she makes clear, is reciprocal.

"In depending upon each other, we want to wish for one another to co-exist, to keep on existing. For example, if you don't wish for blueberries you don't pick them in the summertime. Then the spirit of the blueberry will not come back. So you must keep on using the land to co-exist. And you do it for all the medicines to keep on existing. Because if we stop using it, what are the reasons why they want to keep on existing, existing themselves, the spirits? So they leave. The medicine in the medicine plants is not strong anymore, 'cause we don't believe in it."

Then, at the very end of the afternoon, when we'd used up the gasoline we'd brought for the generators to run our lights and equipment, Lena Nottaway spoke about having lost a foot to diabetes. She is convinced that if she had kept on using her snowshoes (an extension of her feet) instead of switching to a snowmobile, she would still be fully mobile.

THE PRINCIPLES OF MODERN WESTERN SCIENCE AND PHILOSOPHY When the European explorers and fur traders came to Canada in the 17th and 18th centuries, they didn't see the world the way the forebears of Lena Nottaway saw it, nor live in it the same way either. They acted upon the world as they saw it through their philosophies of modern science and utilitarian commerce, and transformed the "new world" to reflect their world view.

Statue of Champlain with Astrolabe, Ottawa

There are many elements involved in the modern scientific world view. Foremost among them is the notion that man is separate from nature. Nature is "other." This concept has its roots in the Christian creation stories, in which man is created in the image of a transcendent God, and given dominion over the natural world. But it became associated with the modern paradigm of natural philosophy through some significant later developments.

One of these is "the invention of linear perspective" (Romanyshyn, 1989:32). Dating from 1435, this way of seeing the world involved removing the seeing "I" (eye) from the living context of the world and placing it behind the framing device of a window. This introduced several changes that Romanyshyn argues were of fundamental importance for the development of modernity. One was that in distancing the self from the living world, the world became an object laid out as a spectacle before the observing eye. A second change was in the new significance of that observing eye as an individual subject with a fixed point of view. A third change was in the abstraction this separation produced, both in the living observer and in what is observed. There was a separation of vision from the other senses, and the novel experience of the eye leaving the body, travelling along the line of sight to the vanishing point and occupying this large field of vision, in a disembodied way. Equally, linear perspective allowed people to see the living world as an object — a landscape, for instance — and as an object to be manipulated once it has been set down on the linear-perspective grid of remote observation.

Linear perspective fit well with other philosophical developments in the mental maps of "modernity," and modern science. One of these, associated with French philosopher, René Descartes, is called Cartesian logic and rationality. It was based on a radical dualism of mind and matter, which helped form the basis of the binary thinking that is itself so central to modern scientific thinking: subject/object, nature/culture, self/other and many more either/or dualisms, with the implication of dominance and subordination built into the pairing.

In England, Isaac Newton developed a whole "mechanical philosophy" associated with the notion that matter is inert and that the power to move matter was not a spiritual property of living matter itself, but a separate force that could be applied to matter. His *Principia* laid out this new world view, this "Newtonian" clockwork universe, animated by knowable, rational laws of motion.

Francis Bacon is sometimes called "the father" of modern science. Partly, perhaps, this is because his scientific ideas, his conception of a modern "way of knowing and doing" (science and technology) had such profound material consequences. His was an applied or practitioners' science. Where the medieval traditions of natural philosophy had sought to know the world as a way to know God, Bacon turned the pursuit of knowledge to new utilitarian goals. His idea was to know nature in order to put nature to practical and profitable use.

"The new man of science must not think that 'the inquisition of nature is in any part interdicted or forbidden.' Nature must be 'bound into service'... and 'moulded' by the mechanical arts. The 'searchers and spies of nature' are to discover her plots and secrets." (Merchant, 1980:169)

His essay, called a "New Atlantis," described a mechanistic utopia run by applied scientists for the benefit of the new propertied middle class of his times. Carolyn Merchant has detected a sexist and even misogynist bias in his writings, with references to the Inquisition of "witches" in essays such as "The Masculine Birth of Time."

Bacon's concept of science also gained prominence because it gained official and lasting state support, in the form of Royal Societies of Science, which Bacon was instrumental in creating. The royal societies gave a very material, and even imperial, grounding to this new way of knowing the world.

Other philosophical influences helped work this way of knowing into a full-fledged modern world view. One of these was **liberalism,** with its focus on individualism. This was expressed as a set of abstract rights and principles: the rights of man (and of women and children only much later); and the rights and privileges of private property, which included the idea of treating the earth as a commodity (e.g., real estate, resources). The rise of **Protestantism** was also important. Not only did this separate the individual from the corporate whole associated with the Catholic church. It also set individuals in a one-to-one relationship with God, in which material self-improvement took on the hue of personal salvation.

Utilitarianism emerged as a new moral philosophy, seeming to blend the ethos of Protestantism with that of liberalism. It extolled a social contract expressed as the greatest happiness for the greatest number, through material progress. It could perhaps be best summed up by an edict from John Locke, one of the founders of liberalism. He defined the modern rational man as "the industrious man who accumulated property."

The modern economic philosophy known as **capitalism** was also a material expression of these ideas. In it, the centre of economic activity shifted from the family/clan home to the anonymous market, and the goal shifted from subsistence to profit-making exchange. As an economic system which came to underpin a whole political and social system, it elevated business and commerce from being, as William Morris put it, "a means to an end to an end in itself."

This modern, scientific, liberal, utilitarian world view conceived of both time and space in entirely new ways. While, for instance, the native world view saw space as an interconnected set of living relationships, this view saw it as inert, as disembodied and reconceptualized as commodities, as real estate and landscape and as matter to be monetarized and moulded. While the native (and generally pre-modern) world view saw time as experience, continuity and ongoing cycles (either climatic or religious), the new world view saw time largely in terms of space: as linear and linked to man-made destiny. The clockwork universe reduced time to units framed by deadlines, and harnessed to commercial contracts.

MODERN SCIENCE AT WORK IN NORTH AMERICA As the video points out, the European newcomers to North America, especially the leaders, or "men in top hats," looked through the lens of this modern philosophy when they journeyed up the St. Lawrence in the 18th and 19th centuries. That lens influenced both what they saw and what they did in response. As Suzanne Zeller points out, modern technological science gave these exploring and entrepreneurial newcomers both the tools for possessing Canada as imperial and personal property, and a mental framework for dignifying this as nation building (see Zeller reading commentary).

But our interest here isn't just in knowing how 18th- and 19th-century empire builders and settlers viewed the world and their place in it, and how this influenced their approach to technology and development in early Canada. It's also to critically understand the approaches to technology and development today. It helps to know, therefore, that there are different approaches associated with different groups with different world views and value systems. It's also good to know that the historical working out of choices isn't a deterministic unfolding of one homogenous mind set over another. It usually involves a struggle, a clash, and sometimes a negotiation and dialectical tension between different and differing mind sets. Difference can make a difference, if it's acknowledged.

Evidence of this struggle historically can be found in the conflict between native conservation traditions vis à vis the land of North America and the newcomers' acquisitive and exploitative ways. Economist and economic historian, Irene Spry, has described this conservation tradition among the Indians on the Canadian Prairie as including knowledge and skills as well as the animals, plants, grasslands, wood and water that the First Peoples depended on for survival. Just as with the English Common Law, the traditional oral law governing the pre-modern English Commons, there were intricate customs associated with who could use what resources within what boundaries. But when the entrepreneurs arrived, particularly on a quest for buffalo hides when these became a staple for conveyor belts in industrial factories, this conservation tradition was destroyed. The newcomers saw the land as "rich with as-yet unappropriated resources," and set about grabbing them. They took them, not for their own subsistence which had limits, but for selling in commercial markets, where there were no limits to growth.

Spry's essay, "The Tragedy of the Loss of the Commons in Western Canada," chronicles many instances of resistance, of native leaders trying to prevent this new exploitation, and some instances of this being respected, and a compromise negotiated. But mostly, the newcomers failed to understand or respect the world view of the native people. Instead, they imposed their ideas of private property and resources there for the taking, and the commons of the Western Prairie was destroyed.

THIS BRINGS US TO THE END of Module I. Its purpose was to introduce technology as a shaping factor in Canada's development and culture, and to open the black box of technology. You were encouraged to consider new ways of thinking about technology critically, as a social construct embodying choices, institutional structures and social values, and also as a force in its own right, limiting or opening up choices, prescribing social relations, or not. The intent of this unit was to introduce the more non-material forces shaping the choice, design and use of technology: values and world view. These are what give certain trends in technology and technological development a seemingly deterministic (some might say "hegemonic") quality, making them seem inevitable, realistic, feasible or progressive.

Think about this in terms of your own knowledge of the world. What comes to mind when you think of progress, either material progress, or the unfolding of the seasons? What comes to mind when you think about time? Leisure time, free time, making good use of time, or "wasting time." All these terms reduce time to units, individualized units of production or consumption, many of them with a utilitarian bent.

It's worth thinking about the enclosing power of mind sets these days when the distinction between culture and nature, between man-made environments and natural ones is blurring and disappearing. The maps, texts and technologies through which the modern "I" represented the world have almost finished transforming it completely. Human and non-human nature have been drawn into that transforming frame, where they are in danger of being reengineered as the extension of modern science-based technology.

This is one of the ideas we'll consider further in the course. But we will consider all the struggles, historical and present, associated with resisting it.

QUESTIONS FOR DISCUSSION

1) Do you think that mindsets and cosmologies can represent a form of mental rigidity in the same way as there were material rigidities built into shipping systems?
2) What is it about native science that makes it more conducive to holistic technological practices rather than prescriptive ones?

COMMENTARY ON SUPPLEMENTARY READINGS

1) Robin Riddington, "From Artifice to Artifact: Stages in the Industrialization of a Northern Hunting People."

This reading provides a nice detailed account of traditional approaches to hunting technology among the Dunne-za Indians of the Peace River region in northern B.C. and Alberta.

* As the title suggests, the native approach to hunting technology emphasized knowledge and know-how (artifice) over tools and technology (artifact).

* For the Dunne-za, the shift in the meaning of technology from artifice to artifact mirrored the actual shift toward dependence on technological artifacts "beyond our control and understanding," and the equally significant shift *away* from traditional technological practice, defined as "an adaptive strategy in which technological knowledge was held by individuals."

* This was a non-material technology, in keeping with the hunter's need to move swiftly over large distances with a minimum of material encumbrance. "Material objects were seen only as the final material connection in the deployment of a strategy held in the mind." A tree branch bent to make a snare, etc.

* This strategy, which was acquired through the oral tradition of learning and honed through personal technological practice, is partly concrete knowledge of the environment and partly a spiritual affinity to the complex interrelationships which constitute that environment. This "animism" and "totemism," plus the techniques for communicating with this animistic realm, called shamanism, are an integral part of native hunting technology.

* There's a difference here between this power of knowing, or medicine power, and simply knowing about something in the sense of possessing knowledge or skill.

* This medicine power, revered by the Dunne-ze as central to their survival, lay in the ability to sense the "mosaic of passages and interactions," in the "life-sustaining network of relationships" not only between animals and the living terrain of earth but between earth, moon, sun and other celestial bodies. Vision quests and dreaming were the traditional media for discovering these trails, and learning how to use them.

* Dreaming, therefore, was central to traditional hunting technology. "Having experienced the pattern of a successful hunt in dream, the hunter knew it was only a matter of time before his trail on earth would catch up to the trail of his dream."

* When the Europeans came, drawing the Dunne-ze into the fur trade with its limitless appetite for furs and constant pressure of

seasonal production targets, the dream was replaced by the rifle as the key hunting technology.

* Equally, the knowledge of dreaming and traditional hunting/survival techniques was displaced by the newly valued knowledge of how to manipulate trade relations with the Europeans.

2) Suzanne Zeller, "Introduction" to *Inventing Canada: Early Victorian Science and the Idea of a Transcontinental Nation.*

This text makes the following important points:

* Modern science became the spearhead of the age of progress. In the process, it displaced art as the dominant language, or cultural mode, of civilization in the modern industrial era.

* Modern science served several utilitarian goals. It provided practical means for solving problems — such as finding arable soils and exploitable minerals. In doing so, it provided a medium for rising above subsistence to real prosperity.

* Two sciences or scientific traditions predominated: the geographical tradition associated with interpreting the physical space of the country in terms of useful resources; and the inventory tradition associated with naming and counting every aspect of that space.

* The statistical movement, with its local and geological surveys, enlisted local settlers in these scientific projects, and in science as a project.

* The utilitarianism of the pursuit of modern science in Canada drew these rational reductionist scientific methods into a larger values framework, lending "a sense of purpose and meaning to the arduous task of settling British North America." Equally, though, the utilitarian framework guaranteed commercial support to scientific projects, such as William Logan's Geological Survey, and scientific support to commercial ventures such as mining.

* The various tools for exploring, mapping and naming the wilderness into rational orderly units carried with them the vision of building an ordered and orderly society.

* The science quest also conveniently masked the crasser pursuit of material gain and political expansion. In other words, science provided not only "the practical means [for colonists] to dominate their physical surroundings but also an ideological framework within which to comprehend the experience of doing so" — as nation building. It provided "an intellectual bridge of common assumptions and aspirations" that compensated for the geographic and other distances among the settler populations.

SOURCES AND FURTHER READINGS

Colorado, Pam, 1988. "Bridging Native and Western Science," *Convergence*, 21(2/3).

Deloria, Vine, 1990. "Traditional Technology," *Winds of Change: Journal of American Indian Engineering and Science*, 5(2).

Fox Keller, Evelyn, 1985. *Reflections on Gender and Science*. Princeton: Princeton University Press.

Gammage, Bill, 1992. "The Achievement of the Australian Aborigines." Occasional Paper no. 1. Honolulu: The Australian and New Zealand Studies Project, School of Hawaiian, Asian and Pacific Studies.

Merchant, Carolyn, 1980. *The Death of Nature*. San Francisco: Harper and Row.

Riddington, Robin, 1983. "From Artifice to Artifact: Stages in the Industrialization of a Northern Hunting People," *Journal of Canadian Studies*, 18(3).

Russell, Bertrand, 1969. *Wisdom of the West*. New York: Crescent Books.

Spry, Irene B. 1983. "The Tragedy of the Loss of the Commons in Western Canada," in *As Long as the Sun Shines and Water Flows*. I. Getty and A. Lussier, eds. Vancouver: U.B.C. Press.

Weatherford, Jack, 1991. *Native Roots: How the Indians Enriched America*. New York: Fawcett Columbine.

Wertheim, Margaret, 1995. "The Way of Logic," *New Scientist* (Dec. 2).

Zeller, Suzanne, 1987. *Inventing Canada: Early Victorian Science and the Idea of a Transcontinental Nation*. Toronto: University of Toronto Press.

MODULE II

TECHNOLOGY AND POLITICAL ECONOMY

OVERVIEW

This module encourages you to take what you've learned about technology as both a social construct and an agent of social development, and apply it to the development of Canada as a modern political economy. It highlights the links between large-scale technological systems and large-scale political economic systems, such as global commodity and labour markets. It also looks at some of the core technologies involved. In the industrial period, these ranged from hydro-electric systems and railways to the beginnings of mass-market advertising. In the current transition to a post-industrial society, the axial technologies are computers and global networks of digital communication, some associated with production, some with distribution and some with marketing and consumption.

Unit 4 will focus on the industrial period, ranging from the 1850s to the 1950s and '60s. It will describe the infrastructures of power and railway transportation, and the kind of development they supported. It will point out the role of government policy, and show how pan-Canadian industrial development dovetailed with a blueprint for nation building within international empires, but controlled by central Canada. It will then critique this view of nation building from the point of view of Canadian economic nationalists, the regions and Quebec.

Unit 5 will look critically at the technological restructuring associated with the current transition from an industrial political economy framed by the nation state to a digital post-industrial economy framed by global markets and global economic institutions. It will also shift the focus somewhat, from the official movers and shakers associated with these systems to the people working inside them. In particular, it will focus on the social relations of work, and what possibilities exist in the new globalized economy for negotiating people's participation in terms of their own particular needs, values and priorities.

OBJECTIVES

At the end of this module, you will have a better understanding of how technology influenced the political and economic development of Canada, and contributed to the tensions within it. In particular you will understand how the bias of communication in the modern era became vested, or embedded, in contemporary infrastructures of transportation, power and telecommunications, and how these vested interests fundamentally biased major political events such as the National Policy and Free Trade. You will also see the link between these large-scale systems and an internationally and pan-national framework of political-economic organization. Finally, it should give you some useful background for critically assessing Canada's and Canadians' options in the political economy of the global village.

CHAPTER 4

TRANSPORTATION SYSTEMS AND EMPIRE BUILDING

This chapter picks up on some of the themes discussed in Unit 1, such as the rigidities built into large-scale technological systems because of the high fixed costs involved. It also extends the theme of how transportation, communication and other technological systems can not only bind a large area, and a large number of people, together. They can also extend unequal relations between centre and margin within that area, through their organizational structures. Thus, terms of trade aren't negotiated as such; they are prescribed through freight-rate structures, etc.

In tracing the industrialization of Canada, we'll note the choice paths available; for instance, between holistic craft production and mass industrial production. We'll also look at the big-business links between, for instance, hydro, railways and staple-resource industries, and the links between these industries and government policy. And we'll see how many of the political issues of our day, such as regional disparities and Quebec separatism, have been strongly influenced by technological developments.

The video includes interviews with Irene Spry, who has researched the history of hydro power and its links to staples industries, with Glen Williams on the subject of free trade and globalization, and with François Rocher, on the subject of Quebec business's links to the separatist cause.

OBJECTIVES

At the end of this unit, you should have a better understanding of the technological backdrop to the economic restructuring occurring in Canada today. You should also be able to identify the various vested interests involved and the conflict of values and priorities at work. And you should be able to answer some of the following questions:

1) How did large-scale hydro power help the development of large-scale resource industries, and visa versa?
2) How was a trans-Canada railway system important to large-scale industry?
3) How did the National Policy serve business interests in the late 19th century and how did free trade serve business interests in the late 20th century?

THE CONNECTION between large-scale transportation systems and empire building through expansionist international markets continued in the move from the mercantile period of economic development to the industrial period. The sailing ship, bringing beaver pelts and timber from the Canadian colonies, was a central motif in the mercantile period. The railway was a central motif of industrialism.

RAILWAYS: MORE THAN A TRANSPORTATION SYSTEM

Eric Hobsbawn argues that, in Britain, the rise of railway transportation was critical in shifting industrialization from its initial craft phase, centred in cottage looms, to a large-scale factory-centred phase. The business of building and running a railway itself represented one of the first of the new large-scale industries. It was also a major market for the new industrial goods of coal, iron and steel. And it provided both a material and financial infrastructure for the expansion of empire, through the export of manufactured goods from "the workshop of the world" to new markets in its colonies. Between 1845 and 1855, Hobsbawn notes, these exports rose at a rate of 7.3 percent a year (Hobsbawn, 1969:109)

100 ton mountain engine, near Field, B.C., 1889. Notman Archives, Montreal

In the emerging country of Canada, entrepreneurs in business and politics tried to use a similar formula in Canadian industrial development. The Confederation (1850-1880) period was one of intense railway investment, with thousands of miles of track laid down in Quebec, Ontario and the Maritimes. As with Britain, the railways themselves became axial industries of the "new industrialism" associated with mass production and mass distribution. As historians Paul Craven and Tom Traves noted, "the railways were Canada's first large-scale integrated industrial corporations." (Craven and Traves, 1987:118) The Grand Trunk Railway, for example, had its own iron foundry, rolling mills and the machinery to produce its own rails. In fact, in the transition period from craft scale to industrial manufacturing, McCalla argues that the railways "were among the largest manufacturing firms in Canada in the period [1850s to '80s], and quite possibly the largest bar none." But at the same time, they were transportation industries, and the bias of space (and commercial empire building) in the modern era was strong.

Equally important was the bias of scale. Railway building required large investments of capital, and knowledge. It's like a canal system, where you can't begin operations until you've dug a complete set of locks between destinations at either end of a waterway. Railways involve investments in track, rights of way, locomotives and cars. They also require coal and water, plus skilled people to operate the route and maintain the equipment. While the transportation system of the fur trade was rigid because of the financial obligations involved — namely the need to pay regular interest on the money advanced to operate this system — the railway system was rigid because money was tied up in the actual technology. Once the money (or overhead investment) was sunk into railway lines and bridges, locomotives and freight cars, the investment was rigid because the capital couldn't be retrieved except through returns on the use of that system. So there was a strong built-in bias to keep using that system. This also meant extending it geographically, to open up new supply sources for the resources and markets for the merchandise it transported. Economies of scale encouraged that bias, as, if you transport a lot of goods over a large market area with a lot of customers, you can spread the overhead costs among more goods and more customers. The lower the cost per unit moved, the more economically feasible it becomes to move cheap goods as well as expensive ones, rather than to make cheap goods only for local markets.

RIGID TECHNOLOGICAL SYSTEMS AND RIGID POLITICAL SYSTEMS The National Policy of 1879 provided major state support to this expansionist bias and to the railway building that embodied it (see box).

First, the policy laid out a continent-wide framework for Canadian economic development, with the major cities along the St. Lawrence River system identified as at the controlling centre of that expansion. It then placed this within the larger frame of international markets, especially for resource staples. Third, it identified domestic industrial development as a complementary (even secondary) activity to staple exports and the transportation infrastructure that would support them. And finally, it tied its tariff policy to this blueprint of development; to resource over-development and industrial under-development.

ELEMENTS OF THE 1879 NATIONAL POLICY

1) the centrality of the St. Lawrence waterway for continental expansion;
2) the reliance on transportation improvements to provide the backbone of this expansion;
3) emphasis on a few staple products for export to European markets;
4) encouragement of developments in finance and secondary industry to complement and support this emphasis;
5) the use of tariffs on imported industrial and manufactured goods to support this too.

(Easterbrook and Aitkin, 1956:388)

It's worth pointing out that the 1872 change to the *Canadian Patent Act,* under which foreign technologies could be granted a Canadian patent, was an important adjunct to the National Policy. It allowed American companies to license their technology to Canadian manufacturers, or to set up branch plants in Canada, in what became known as "industrialization by invitation" to international business interests.

Where there had been a nucleus of Canadian-based manufacturing in train and railway building, this choice path was marginalized in favour of rapid pan-national development, through a combination of Canadian infrastructure developments supporting resource exports and merchandise imports, plus foreign technology and branch-plant investment in manufacturing. With this, the National Policy helped to marginalize the choice path of intensive locally based development, geared to the smaller-scale units of villages, small towns and craft manufacturing. On a more philosophical and ideological level, the policy helped to marginalize development as community building in favour of development as commercial-systems and empire building, and to consolidate the European-centred values, and assumptions about progress associated with it, as "Canadian" values and ideals.

The social histories that have emerged since the 1960s, on labour history, community history, women's history, native history, the story of ordinary people and the business of how they made ends meet, have confirmed that development is a social construct, and even a social struggle, with many paths left in the shadows while the dominant themes moved ahead. In many of these micro- rather than macro-focused histories, we can detect glimmerings of the nation-building-as-community-building theme. As one example, Metis writer, Howard Adams, offers a retelling of the 1885 Northwest Rebellion, or Riel Rebellion, in which he describes an emerging alliance between the local native people and the white settlers. He mentions Henry Jackson, a white farmer who "worked closely with the native people's movement. Together with Charles Adams, president of the English Halfbreeds' Association, Thomas Scott, a white farmer and others, Jackson helped organize the Settlers' and Farmers' Unions throughout the Northwest."

Part of the struggle was to get Ottawa to recognize these locally elected organizations as the basis for legitimate local, multi-racial, multi-cultural government in the Northwest. Instead, Adams argues, the Prime Minister used the local newspaper, which he'd acquired six months previously, to break up the partnership between native and white people and to discredit the leaders of the local-democracy movement. The situation moved toward confrontation, the outcome of which was decisive. "The new rulers established capitalism in the Northwest, and the way was clear for modern agriculture and industrialism to expand through the private enterprise system"(Adams,1989:70).

ELECTRICITY: MORE THAN JUST A POWER LINE

Geographically, the industrial development path followed the two lines of Canadian infrastructure investment: railway lines plus hydro-electric lines. Telegraph lines might possibly be added as a third. An adjunct to railway building, and generally following the railway rights-of-way, telegraph communication was critically important for large-scale industrial coordination. It was also critical to the development of mass-circulation newspapers during this period of industrial development. Their large-circulation ads helped consolidate the mass-production model of industrialization as it linked mass production and mass distribution to mass consumption (see Unit 7).

The 1880s were a critical period of technological change, when craft-scale manufacturing powered by hand, foot and water was superseded by industrial mass production powered by electricity. The scale of production associated with this phase of industrialization was useful to the large-scale distribution systems associated with the railway. Because production vastly exceeded the capacity of local markets to absorb it, it had to be distributed further afield. Large-scale power systems were crucial in this scale-up. Not surprisingly, some of the leading entrepreneurs in transportation became involved in hydro development.

There are many similarities between hydro development and railway development. Both involved tools and technologies combined into a centrally controlled technological system (see the discussion of Thomas Edison in Chapter 2). Both involved large initial investments, and monopoly-scale corporate organization became a solution to the financial insecurities these large fixed investments involved. Both were rigid systems in that the financial investments were fixed, literally in concrete in the case of hydro dams. Both incorporated a strong bias toward business priorities, and gained government support. And both were major industries in their own right. In 1932, the total value of capital invested in generating stations was greater than that invested in any other industry in Canada (Biss(Spry), 1936:228). In that year, a full third of Canada's hydro power was absorbed by one resource industry, pulp and paper. Thanks to the staple infrastructure industries of railways and hydro, by 1950 pulp and paper had become Canada's leading industry, accounting for 24 percent of exports in an economy that still viewed international trade and related expansion as a central measure of economic health and vigour.

The video interview with Irene Spry emphasizes the tie-in between large-scale resource-staple industries, such as pulp and paper and metal refining, and the large-scale power systems needed to run them. She makes the point that these industries virtually demanded the kind of large-scale infrastructure that only a large organization like Ontario Hydro can provide. She also makes the point that, as a public utility, Hydro was able to support community priorities plus business priorities.

However, it's worth reflecting back on the fork in the technological-choice road in the early 1900s. A provincial network of municipal power organizations might have struck a better balance between community priorities and those of big business. This might have slowed Ontario Hydro's rush into nuclear energy in the early 1960s. Perhaps it might also have forestalled the inequities that saw 40 percent of Ontario homes electrified by the 1920s (mostly in urban centres), while many rural communities waited until the 1940s and '50s for modern conveniences.

Such an organizational model could also have affected the distribution of social power as it distributed the control of an important technological infrastructure across the "margins" of small municipalities as well as the large urban centres. It's worth reflecting on the parallels between a multitude of community networks and usegroups forming the backbone of the Internet versus a few big service providers. But then, as now, this would also depend on the values and world view of the people involved

CHALLENGING THE DISCOURSE There is little discussion of these conflicts and choices in mainstream stories of Canadian development. Mostly, it's a linear account of forward-thinking individuals, primarily moneyed and propertied Anglo-Saxon men who managed development rather than worked physically themselves (see box).

> "The history of the Canadian Pacific Railroad is primarily the history of the spread of Western civilization over the northern half of the North American continent. The addition of technical equipment described as [the] physical property of the Canadian Pacific Railway Company was a cause and an effect of the strength and character of that civilization."
> (Innis, 1971:287)

There was no discussion of the unequal relations involved, and the price associated with the depletion of fur-bearing animals, forests, fish and minerals, and the dependency on American technology. For a while, too, expansionist economic development appeared to deliver its benefits to what seemed to be the majority. In the 1960s, however, the pronouncements of Canadian philosopher, George Grant, caught the attention of an emerging generation of post-war economic nationalists. It sparked a sustained critique of technology, the progress myth, and modernity in general, and American domination of the Canadian economy in particular.

A number of studies documented the extent of American ownership of Canadian industry, especially in resources and manufacturing (Levitt, 1970). Others examined the state of Canadian technological dependence and the under-development or truncated development of Canadian industry. Political scientist, Glen Williams, points out that Canadian branch plants were often forced to license production technology, even though it was often old or nearly obsolete, from the American parent company, and were mandated to produce for the Canadian domestic market only.

George Grant's analysis went deeper than this. The first stage was a critique of Canadian political developments. In *Lament for a Nation*, he interpreted the defeat of Conservative leader John Diefenbaker in the 1963 federal election as the end of nation building as grounded in the building of particular communities in Canada. He saw the triumph of liberalism in that election as representing the triumph of American corporate values and the end of any hope that Canada could chart a destiny separate from that commercial empire. Equally important was the post-election re-engineering of the Conservative Party. It moved away from its old community-based tradition of upholding the collective public good toward a new philosophy of economic liberalism. Grant's lament was for the demise of any political economic project other than building bigger and faster production, distribution and consumption systems. All that was left was to emulate the American corporate and consumer system, where human rights are defined as access to technology and human well being is measured by the standard-of-living index.

George Grant. William Christian

His political analysis evolved into a more philosophical analysis, described in later books such as *Technology and Empire*. His view shifted from the particulars of the American commercial empire to the more general "ontological" concept of an "empire of technique." We've been colonized not only as a nation, he said, but as a society, and can only think in terms of technical rationality (see Unit 6 for more discussion of this position).

"The aspirations of progress [material progress, through technology] have made Canada redundant." (Grant, 1986:53)

George Grant, with his deep and religious conservatism, was an unlikely hero for the 1960s economic nationalists to adopt. But his Loyalist bias against the US made him a convenient ally for those (notably those in central Canada) who preferred not to confront empire building within Canada itself.

EMPIRE BUILDING WITHIN CANADA The Maritime provinces embraced the National Policy as a tool for pan-Canadian nation building along the lines envisaged by the Fathers of Confederation. Enough money and knowledge had been accumulated during the sailing era from timber and fish exports and boat building to foster a major development of local, and locally owned, manufacturing in the 1880s. In cooperative joint ventures, local monied families built textile mills, sugar refineries and steel mills, drawing on local coal and iron-ore supplies and using the Inter-Colonial Railway as a market-distribution system.

But the lines also brought manufactured goods from central Canada. In fact, of the nearly $16 million in interregional commerce generated in 1885, 70 percent of the traffic was from central Canada to the Maritimes (Acheson et al.,1985:11). Maritime business interests argued that railways, built at public expense, should be run as "vehicles of nationhood ..., promoting national economic integration rather than as commercial institutions." The freight rates charged on the Inter-Colonial were pricing Maritime products out of the markets of central Canada, and many of these businesses started to fail.

But the problems went deeper than this. Economies of scale dictated that central Canadian industries be run on a scale that could supply the entire Canadian market. The Maritime manufacturers favoured a national trade association to regulate production and market shares. This failed partly because of Maritimers' suspicion of central Canadian businessmen and partly because these businessmen were already buying up local businesses, and sometimes shutting them down. A brief initial period of industrial development in the Maritimes was followed by a steady de-industrialization. Maritime businessmen moved their money to central Canada, the Maritime banks followed suit and the region lapsed into an unequal relation with central Canada, fostered by key infrastructures such as the railway and the financial system, which would later foist a similar underdevelopment on the West.

> "Western Canada has paid for the development of Canadian nationality, and it would appear that it must continue to pay. The acquisitiveness of eastern Canada shows little sign of abatement." (Innis, 1971:294)

In much the same vein, Harold Innis wrote about the CPR's effect on Western Canada in terms of the inequalities imposed through freight rates and the Western distribution of goods (see box).

QUEBEC NATIONALISM In Quebec's Quiet Revolution of the 1960s, a good deal of attention focused on language and culture, and the need to preserve and protect Quebec sovereignty in these areas. In the midst of this, René Lévesque (a member of Jean Lesage's reformist Liberal government of the 1960s) initiated the nationalization of Quebec's hydro-electric industry. Hydro Quebec, and the megaprojects associated with building its technological infrastructure, became a major motor of a Quebec-based industrial development. It also became a powerful symbol of the "maître chez nous" project of Quebec nationalism. Through the businesses it supported by giving contracts to build and run its mega-power projects, it fostered a new generation of Quebec business leaders. This was not the old guard working for the English-Canadian bosses of branch plants, such as Imperial Tobacco Co. in Montreal, but a new elite already operating in the continental arena which had been steadily opening since the Second World War and the Auto Pact. François Rocher has argued that "support for free trade is a function of the nature of the markets" in which various companies and businesses operated (Rocher, 1991:150).

Furthermore, this tie-in between the old English establishment and protectionism, from which the younger generation of Quebecois business leaders distanced themselves, added a nationalist glow to the free trade discussions in Quebec. Free trade became associated with the notion of an independent Quebec taking its place confidently in the new globalizing world economy free trade was creating. The contradictions remained hidden beneath a seemingly common front of Quebec nationalist support of free trade.

COMMENTARY ON SUPPLEMENTARY READINGS

1) Neil Bradford and Glen Williams, "What Went Wrong? Explaining Canadian Industrialization," in *The New Canadian Political Economy.*

This article describes Canadian industrialization as featuring technological dependence, a warped industrial structure, pitiful exports of manufactured products contributing to a chronic trade deficit in this area, and high levels of foreign ownership. It then explains this situation, making the following points:

* Overall, it can be explained: 1) by interpreting Canadian industrialization within a larger international framework; 2) by seeing it as a social construct with different institutions and groups exercising various degrees of influence; 3) by seeing it in terms of historical continuities, with one set of choices influencing subsequent choices; and 4) by seeing manufacturing as part of a dialectical relationship of development vis à vis resource industries, which took precedence.

* Innis' strength was that he took an international and historical view, interpreting industrialization as a balancing act between ongoing staples exports to the British empire and a pan-Canadian consolidation to resist integration into the American empire.

* Mel Watkins filled in some of the gaps left by Innis in stressing the importance of agency and choice, particularly among the local financial elites who could have chosen to channel profits from staples extraction into domestic development, thus avoiding the "staples trap."

* Extending this idea, Nelles' work on the "manufacturing condition" in Ontario demonstrates that local business interests, with the support of Ontario Hydro, could get a province, if not the federal government, to legislate against the interests of American capital.

* Similarly, Richards and Pratt have shown that the province, with the support of a "regional bourgeoisie," can build more value-added development on to staples, such as oil and potash, and again avoid the staples trap.

* McCallum's research demonstrates the importance of competitive transportation systems to help local businesses succeed.

* Levitt and Watkins' work on foreign ownership underscores the importance of interpreting Canadian development in a larger international framework. They argue that Canada has been "recolonized" through a systematic takeover of key industries, which cumulatively prevents Canada from charting its own development.

* Naylor noted that Canada's business elites worked out complementary strategies of development with international business interests. Their strategic investments in transportation and other

infrastructures leveraged foreign investment for staples exports, and later, "industrialization by invitation."

* Williams emphasizes that little has changed over the years, with business logic driving rationalization of regional production centres into a continental economy.

* Theorists taking other social actors into account have argued that labour supported branch-plant industrialization because it delivered secure full-time employment. Similarly, in Quebec, the business elites, the cultured middle class and organized labour rallied together in support of provincial initiatives to increase francophone control over the local economy and use provincial policy to develop it more fully.

*Mahon has shown how unions by themselves can't necessarily get state support for their agenda. When protective tariffs were being dismantled, in the interests of resource industries over manufacturing, the textile and clothing unions tried, unsuccessfully, to get state support for a corporatist planning solution.

2) Ursula Franklin, Chapter 5, *The Real World of Technology*.

Here, Franklin demonstrates the shaping power of technological infrastructures, making the following points:

* Prescriptive technologies represent a generalized infrastructure underpinning and directing the "culture of compliance" prevailing in contemporary technological society.

* Infrastructures take time to develop, and are associated with later stages of technological development when certain designs and uses of a new technology become standardized and set down in technological systems.

* This standardization/consolidation phase explains the strange reversal that seems to go on in the cycle of technological change: from the excitement associated with the initial innovation (mechanical-bride) phase to the later stage where individuals are confined at best to multiple choices and are even "enslaved" by the technological system.

* Feminist scholars have studied the social-structuring power of these infrastructures, and have described the prevailing male pattern of them to be "hierarchial, authoritarian, competitive and exclusive." Not surprisingly, many of these infrastructures also pack a strong gender and racial bias, not to mention a disabling one.

* By contrast, a lot of women's work, including that in the home, historically and at present is distinguished by its lack of a rigid infrastructure. Instead it's holistic, relying heavily on informed personal judgement and understanding of both the work as a whole and a sensitivity to the particulars of different circumstances. Although

these strengths aren't valued by the technological world order, Franklin considers them central to a people-centred rethinking of technology.

* What's valuable in these histories is retrieving the choice path where engaged personal and social relations (and the engaged innovation that emerged within those social bonds) were at the centre of technology before rigid prescriptive systems and infrastructures took over.

* There's more than material structures and cost structures involved in these rigid infrastructures. There is also knowledge, including common knowledge and popular (internalized) assumptions about what and who is important, and what and who is not. (This is discussed more in Unit 9, as "cultural monopolies of knowledge.")

QUESTIONS FOR DISCUSSION

1) What structural factors propelled the development of hydro power and rail transportation along similar lines? What were some of the key institutions involved?
2) How did hydro power, rail transportation and industrial mass production complement each other's development? What priorities did they have in common?
3) What's the connection between large-scale systems and infrastructures and empire building?

SOURCES AND FURTHER READINGS

Acheson, T., Frank, D. and Frost, J., 1985. *Industrialization and Underdevelopment in the Maritimes, 1880-1930*. Toronto: Garamond Press.

Adams, Howard, 1989. *Prison of Grass*. Saskatoon: Fifth House.

Armstrong, C. and Nelles, H.V., 1986. *Monopoly's Moment: The Organization and Regulation of Canadian Utilities, 1830-1930*. Philadelphia: Temple University Press.

Biss (Spry), Irene, 1936. "Hydro-electric Power," in *Encyclopedia of Canada*, Vol. 3. Toronto: University Associates of Canada.

Bradford, N. and Williams, G., 1989. "What Went Wrong? Explaining Canadian Industrialization," in *The New Canadian Political Economy*. Wallace Clement and Glen Williams, eds. Montreal/Kingston: McGill-Queen's University Press.

Craven, Paul and Traves, Tom, 1987. "Canadian Railways as Manufacturers, 1850-1880," in *Perspectives in Canadian Economic History*, ed. Douglas McCalla. Toronto: Copp Clark.

Easterbrook, W.T. and Aitkin, H.G.J., 1956. *Canadian Economic History*. Toronto: Macmillan.

Grant, George, 1986. *Lament for a Nation: The Defeat of Canadian Nationalism*. Ottawa: Carleton University Press.

Grant, George, 1969. *Technology and Empire*. Toronto: House of Anansi.

Hobsbawn, Eric, 1969. *Industry and Empire*. Hammondsworth: Penguin.

Innis, Harold, 1971. *A History of the Canadian Pacific Railway*. Toronto: University of Toronto Press.

Levitt, Kari, 1970. *Silent Surrender*. Toronto: MacMillan.

McCalla, Douglas, 1993. *Planting the Province: The Economic History of Upper Canada, 1784-1870*. Toronto: University of Toronto Press.

McKay, Paul, 1983. *Electric Empire: The Inside Story of Ontario Hydro*. Toronto: Between the Lines.

Rocher, Francois, 1991. "Canadian Business, Free Trade and the Rhetoric of Economic Continentalization," *Studies in Political Economy*, 35 (Summer).

Williams, Glen, 1987. *Not for Export: Toward a Political Economy of Canada's Arrested Industrialization*. Toronto: McClelland and Stewart.

CHAPTER 5

INSIDE THE NETWORKS OF THE GLOBAL ECONOMY

OVERVIEW

This chapter moves the discussion of Canada's political economy forward to the present. It shifts the focus from the technological systems of the industrial period to the computer-communication systems of the post-industrial era. It also turns the frame of reference around somewhat. Instead of viewing these systems from the outside, and in terms of the institutions that built them, it looks at them from the inside. In particular, it pays attention to the people who work for and within the computerized structures of the new economy. It provides some historical backdrop to this perspective too. It traces the changing social relations of work from the craft period through industrialization to, now, the computerization of work in the post-industrial economy. Related to this, it also traces the gradual depersonalization of work and the control of work, and how this changes with the digital economy.

It builds on some of Ursula Franklin's ideas we've discussed earlier: especially the difference between holistic and prescriptive technology, and the link between prescriptive technologies and a culture of compliance. It also harks back to the previous discussion about values and world view.

In this chapter we also apply some of Marshall McLuhan's insights, including his more pessimistic thoughts about the enclosure of people inside the technostructures of the digital universe.

We'll also consider George Grant's ideas about technology as an all-pervasive world view, symbolized by the dynamo image. And we'll consider the dynamo as a generalized environment for getting and doing work, and taking care of business.

The video also draws on a student discussion about personal experiences working in the computerized work world, and ends with a panel discussion about the problems facing working people in the post-industrial economy.

OBJECTIVES

When you have finished this unit, you should be able to explore, if not answer, some of the following questions:

1) What impact has technological restructuring had on employment and work?
2) How do the structures of the new workplace and cultural training programs like TQM create a "culture of compliance"?
3) How has the organization and control of work changed since the days of craft production?

THE PRIMARY FOCUS here is on the social relations of work, and how these have changed in the development of first industrial and, now, the post-industrial economy. It's useful, however, to understand the core technologies underpinning this revolutionary restructuring of social and political relations.

THE TECHNOLOGIES INVOLVED

Everything we've discussed so far about infrastructures and fundamental approaches to technology and development apply here. In a sense they come to fruition here as well. In the industrial age, the key infrastructures were electric power systems and related mass-production systems, plus the mass-distribution systems of the railway and, later, trucks. The first infrastructures of mass-communication, including mass-circulation newspapers and telegraph lines, were also important, and gained added importance over time.

In the restructuring associated with the shift to the post-industrial digital economy, mass-communication infrastructures become paramount. Mass-transportation, hydro power and large-scale production systems are still important. But most of these are being redefined by the communication infrastructures, almost as adjuncts to them.

It's not just communication technology, however. It's communication integrated with computer technology, specifically through the microchip, invented in 1972. The chip miniaturized computer power so that it was practical to computerize almost every mechanical process. This included communications, with the addition of automated switching, monitoring and rate-calculation systems. It automated industrial production, through robots, scanning, and other "smart" devices. But even more important, it automated paperwork, filing and other administrative functions, everywhere from offices to labs to stores and schools.

Robots at CAMI auto assembly plant from *Working Lean*, by Laura Sky. Canadian Auto Workers

The first phase of this involved upgrading mechanical equipment with computer controls. The second phase involved the integration of various computers and computerized machines to create production sub-systems and office sub-systems integrated in turn with management-information systems.

Gradually, the connecting lines of communication became a bigger and bigger part of the picture. More and more systems of production and information became integrated into ever larger networks of digital communication. And with this, a fundamental shift occurred in how organizations were structured and managed.

Instead of being defined in terms of fixed industrial production sites, they were increasingly reorganized around global digital networks. Corporations were no longer unified around fixed smokestacks. In the post-industrial era, they are increasingly unified around flexible information networks: largely invisible ones consisting of fibre-optic cable, satellite plus conventional phone and cable lines popularly known as the Information Highway.

The term, "information highway," was coined by US vice-president Al Gore in 1993 when he introduced his $2billion-a-year National Information Infrastructure Program, a sequel to his 1980s *High Performance Computing Act*, geared to retooling US industry with super-fast computers and networks "to enable this country to leapfrog the Japanese."(Coy, 1991) As in Canada, where the federal government launched a similar information-infrastructure boosting program in 1994 through a largely private-sector consortium called CANARIE, "economic renewal" has been the priority. From the outset, too, the focus has been on business as well as on multi-media marketing, distribution or even teleshopping. A 1994 publication, *The Canadian Information Highway: Building Canada's Information and Communications Infrastructure*, was unequivocal. "The key to competitiveness will be the ability of firms to develop, acquire and adapt ... the tools that will be available on and through the information highway." (Industry Canada, 1994:8)

Through the Information Highway, various production sites (the former smokestacks and other bricks-and-mortar structures where people work) can be integrated into companies' networks according to current production priorities, then dis-integrated as these priorities change.

"Agile" production and "flexible accumulation" are hallmarks of this new economy.

THE CHANGING ORGANIZATION OF WORK Looking at the organization of work historically is useful for recalling how embedded the social relations of work used to be. They were part of the work process itself and the particular people involved. In craft production, the work was done holistically, with the worker fully involved, head and hand, in guiding and conducting the work. But it wasn't just a question of scale. It was also a question of values: the valuing of personal participation and involvement, of reciprocity and personal autonomy. The late 19th-century poet and interior designer, William Morris, argued that craft production, compared to the emerging mass-production industrialization of his day, involved a different world view and logic. It wasn't the logic of economic efficiency. It was a social logic associated with what William Morris called "the doing of a thing duly"(see box).

> In the heyday of craftsmanship, "the unit of labour was an intelligent man. Under this system of handiwork, no great pressure of speed was put on a man's work, but he was allowed to carry it through leisurely and thoughtfully; it used the whole of a man for the production of a piece of goods, and not small portions of many men; it developed the workman's whole intelligence... Even the simplest of crafted products shared in the meaning and emotion of the intellectual. One melted into the other by scarce perceptible gradations; in short, the best artist was a workman still, the humblest workman was an artist." (Morris, 1993:29)

As commercial values rose in prominence, so did large-scale prescriptive systems; each, in fact, supported and complemented the other. As discussed earlier, in terms of the technological infrastructure of the fur trade, these systems served as the conduit for advancing what Harold Innis called "the penetrative powers of the pricing system." Anticipating our discussion of McLuhan, they were the medium to the message of commercial industrial development and success measured as material achievement.

THE DEPERSONALIZATION OF WORK Head work was separated from hand work in an increasingly complex division of labour, and in increasingly large-scale units of production. With this division, labour relations between the "head" man and the "hands" or hands-on workers became more depersonalized. This change, which had more to do with values than with industrial technology or its absence, applied as much to agriculture as to industry. Large factory-scale farms of the 19th century joined the general shift away from the feudal tradition of commitments to workers, and their families, over a lifetime and even from one generation to another. Instead, large farmers started laying off idle hands, in keeping with the new utilitarian view of workers as units of labour power, or commodities (Langdon, 1975:4-5).

Along with this depersonalization, human labour, skills and involvement were steadily displaced by machine power and calculating ability. Human judgement and principled decision making was also taken over by bureaucratic and other machinery, with workers' decision making limited to technical adjustments and trouble shooting.

TOWARD COMPUTERIZED CONTROL Control over work shifted from the personal control and autonomy of holistic craft production to variations on remote control associated with prescriptive production systems. Partly, this was because management owned and controlled the means of production, as technology increasingly took the form of large-scale industrial equipment. Bosses in front offices told workers in the back what to do. Over time, however, direct personal involvement was replaced by the more depersonalized management of bureaucracy and assembly lines. Computerized production and management systems have completed the depersonalization and at the same time brought it full circle (see the section on cultural training later in this chapter).

POST FORDISM Work and working have changed dramatically since Henry Ford invented the assembly line and the idea of mainstream mass-produced cars for mainstream American families, and helped set in place what became known as the Fordist social contract. It featured stable and relatively high levels of employment at decent wages, which in turn supported mass consumption in fairly stable national economies. It was also regulated in the public interest through a combination of strong unions and decent labour standards and legislation, with state-funded social programs such as unemployment and welfare providing a "social safety net" for those in need.

This social contract certainly didn't embrace everyone; women and racial and ethnic minorities faced much more precarious employment and worked in less than well-regulated environments. Nonetheless, it was the basis of a broad social consensus about development, technological "progress" and the public good.

The terms of that contract have now changed. First, technological restructuring has transformed national machine-based economies into a global systems-based one. Second, government spending cuts and down sizing have diminished the government's role as regulator and shredded the social safety net. Furthermore, these developments clear the path for minimized global labour standards achieved through global corporate regulation, without interference by local national governments.

The new social landscape has the following characteristics:

1) high levels of unemployment, as more and more goods and services are produced, and distributed, with a minimum of human involvement, and as customers and consumers take on work (as self-service) which people used to be paid to do for them.

2) high levels of underemployment, as automated sub-systems, and expert-level software and smart networks replace human intelligence, knowledge and involvement. Full-time people everywhere from factories to hospitals to offices of all kinds are being replaced with part-time people. The middle ranks of workers are being decimated. This was first documented in a 1986 study by Statistics Canada, and has been further explored through studies on disparities in hours of work and income.

A 1994 study charted a dramatic shift of people into "non-standard" forms of work through the 1980s. Notably too, even among people with post-secondary education and at least one university

Net Change in full-time equivalent jobs, 1981-86 by occupation and wage level (thousands)

	Clerical	Prof./ Tech.	Mgt./ Admin.	Sales	Service	Primary	Manufac-turing
>$6.76	+13	+17	+52	+63	+135	—	+17
$6.77 -9.22	-74	-16	+34	—	-5	+6	-64
$9.23 -$11.87	-51	+10	+39	+15	+12	+14	-63
$11.88 -$15.58	-10	+82	+64	+21	+22	+32	-17
<$15.59	-30	+83	+94	+25	+17	+8	-53

high growth (>15,000)
low growth (<15,000 + under)
net job loss or flat

Source: *Wages and Jobs in the 1980s: Changing Youth Wages and the Declining Middle.* Statistics Canada, July 1988

degree, men— particularly those under the age of 40 — shifted dramatically from full-time employment to either part-time or contract work (Morissette and Sunter, 1994). In 1996, the national unemployment rate for young people (aged 15-24) was 17 percent. Furthermore, a 1997 report (Statistics Canada's Labour Force Survey) noted that employment opportunities of any kind were so bad that 40 percent of young people reported having no work experience to date in 1996, compared to only 18 percent with no work experience in 1989.

3) A third major development is societal polarization: dramatic new inequalities of income, occupational status, access to technology (at home, for instance) and level of involvement. In the work environment, it's a polarization between the over-worked rich, who often work well over a 50-hour work week to keep up with the new standards of performance, and the barely working or out-of-work poor, who work 30 hours a week at most. There's also a polarization between those who work with the powerful new networked digital systems, and those who merely work for them — as the fast-flying fingers inputting data, as the voice with the smile at the other end of a 1-800 number.

I've described these people as the human equivalent of post-it notes to suggest something of their marginal and irrelevant status (Menzies, 1996:10). They're merely flesh and blood skill sets stuck on briefly, then discarded without a sound or a trace of their presence.

McLUHAN'S INSIGHTS Marshall McLuhan's writings are useful for their insider's insights into the human experience of this new technological order. Fascinated by technology as a kind of material grammar organizing society, he argued that the techniques of fragmentation, so central to machine technology, were the organizational grammar of the industrial age. Its extreme form is military organization where "large amounts of homogenized energies" were concentrated into one rigidly organized fighting machine (McLuhan, 1964:76).

Marshall McLuhan. Barbara Wilde

McLuhan has been tagged as a technological optimist largely because he predicted that computers would liberate people from the fragmented tasks of industrialism. He envisaged an age in which everyone was integrated into the networked world of computers, bypassing mere jobs in favour of "complex roles." The key, he felt was electricity, which was instant and ubiquitous, and could unite all the previously fragmented mechanical bits of industrial production into an organic interrelated whole. "It is this electric speed-up and interdependence that has ended the assembly line in industry.... Hence the folly of alarm about unemployment," he wrote, confidently, in 1964. "Paid learning is already becoming both the dominant employment and the source of new wealth in our society. This is the new role for men in society..."(McLuhan, 1964:304).

McLuhan's sexist language is worth noting; it alerts us to question some of McLuhan's sweeping assumptions.

TECHNOLOGY AS EXTENSION/AUTO-AMPUTATION We should look at McLuhan's assumptions about technology as an extension of "man." He meant the simulated extension of the senses, of the mind, of the foot, etc. He assumed that if it worked for one, it could work for all. In other words, the computer could function as an extension of everyone's mind and consciousness. But in a typical McJob work situation, the computer is hardly an extension of the operator's mind, or an expression of that person's values. The new digital work environment is governed by the "cybernetics of labour"(Haraway, 1991:161). The computer system controls and monitors the work being done. It's rigidly constructed to make support-staff workers function as an extension of the dictates which management has programmed into the computerized work situation.

> "By continuously embracing technologies, we relate ourselves to them as servomechanisms. That is why we must, to use them at all, serve these objects, these extensions of ourselves, as gods or minor religions. An Indian is the servomechanism of his canoe, as the cowboy of his horse or the executive of his clock." (McLuhan, 1964:55)

Ironically, McLuhan's insights into how a technological extension of a sense will cause a simultaneous amputation of other senses and organs is extremely helpful here. My own research into how technological restructuring is affecting people suggests that people's capacity to think and act for themselves is actually being amputated when they're enclosed in a technologically defined work space. They are so hemmed in by the corporate definition of work, projected by the system, that they become involuntary ***servo-mechanisms*** of it.

A ***servo-mechanism*** is a self-governing, self-activating mechanical device that's part of a larger system, such as a home-heating system. The thermostat is a servo-mechanism in that it will switch the furnace on when the house temperature drops below a pre-programmed point, and turn it off once it's reached a pre-set maximum. The idea of people becoming involuntary servo-mechanisms of vast global production systems is disturbing. Yet there is evidence of this happening. Again, McLuhan's evocative writing is useful here, in particular his retelling of the Greek legend of Narcissus. The key here is closure.

In the story, Narcissus catches a glimpse of himself in a pool of water and thinks it is another person. He starts to wave and gesture back and forth with himself. He's locked into that continuous feedback loop, and does not realize that he's closed inside the universe of his gaze. The nymph, Echo, tries to restore his perspective by bringing him back to his other senses, such as hearing. But she can't break the spell. Narcissus is locked in, totally enclosed.

Similarly, in the world of work, as people work in isolated work cubicles in call centres, or as teleworkers at home, or even sometimes as the single operative on an integrated work station in a factory, they too get closed in. The computerized work environment provides the entire context of their work. It defines and controls every aspect of the work to be done. It monitors every aspect of its performance. Then it provides feedback on that performance in strictly computer terms — x items processed per shift and so on. Without other reference points through which to reorient themselves, people can become hooked on meeting or beating the numbers. The excerpt from the film *Working Lean* and from the student discussion on the video should help to illustrate this. As Ursula

Franklin points out, prescriptive systems are "designs for compliance," and all the more totalizing as they enclose people in their pace and scale and logic.

CULTURAL TRAINING As mentioned earlier, computerized production and management systems have completed the depersonalization of work. People work less and less with each other, or even for a particular boss. Increasingly, they work for and within technological systems. But the sense of alienation or auto-amputation people might have is mitigated by the new management communications programs associated with "Total Quality Management" or TQM. These actively encourage workers to identify with the company and the goals the technological systems epitomize. They bring the depersonalization of work full circle by putting people back in touch with who they're working for. It's a simulated personal relationship, achieved through corporate "communications" sessions which can range from meetings with sales representatives and involvement in productivity-improvement teams to pep rallies and free t-shirts, hats and company mugs. They're largely a Japanese management philosophy for cultivating employee loyalty and being part of the corporate team.

It remains to be seen whether or not a new tribal-like corporate bonding will emerge as the new social pattern, as McLuhan predicted (with corporate slogans and mission statements at work complementing the bonding activities of television). Meanwhile, the repersonalization of work through TQM and other programs seems to fit McLuhan's prediction about a reversal of tendencies from the industrial era of fragmentation to the electric/electronic era of organic integration. But it will take a lot to counter the continuing fragmentation and disintegration of work occurring in the move toward contracting out, increased part-time, temporary and other contingent work, and the fundamental alienation of people's mental and physical labour.

GRANT'S INSIGHTS George Grant would feel that his prophecies of the late 1960s were being fulfilled in the late 1990s as people talk about being driven by the out-performance standards of technological systems. Cathy Austin, the woman in the excerpt from *Working Lean,* was used to the hard work demanded by the family farm, where she was known and valued as a person, and the farm's work had limits set by acreage and the seasons. But in the new work environment, a global joint venture between a Japanese and an American auto company, there were no limits in space, nor, it seemed in time. She had all the marks of having been turned into a servo-mechanism of a technological system large enough to be called a dynamo.

The term ***technological dynamo*** is derived from the Greek word for power. Its use here harks back to the steam-based power generators used to run factories and other mechanical operations in the 19th century. These massive engines came to epitomize the modern age of machinery, and were seen as a potent symbol of progress by enthusiasts. The 680-ton Corliss steam engine which ran all the exhibits in the Machinery Hall at the 1876 Philadelphia Centennial Exposition reportedly stole the show. As William Leiss has written, "it so outstripped the capacity of ordinary descriptive reporting that only ecstatic metaphorical construction could register reactions to it.... 'The machine emerged as a kind of fabulous automaton — part animal, part machine, part god'."(Leiss, 1990:36)

Grant's concern was that the logic of the machine and expansionist systems building would come to monopolize thinking, not just in the workplace but everywhere except in the remotest recesses of people's private thoughts. People would no longer need bosses driving them to turn out more widgets, or more pizzas, or more telephone sales faster and faster. People would drive themselves. All other meanings of work — being engaged with others, in a community of known fellow workers or in providing services to members of the public, or making a good meal for someone, etc. — have been stripped away by the depersonalization of work, the fragmentation of work, the disintegration of human involvement and the reintegration of people as isolated operatives in vast technological networks.

> "We live then in the most realized technological society which has yet been....Yet the very substance of our existing which has made us the leaders in technique, stands as a barrier to any thinking which might be able to comprehend technique from beyond its own dynamism." (Grant, 1969:40)

THE DISCOURSE ON TECHNOLOGY The *discourse* on technology mirrors this concentration of meaning around the technological imperative, which suggests that it has the same biases built into it. As an organized and largely prescriptive system of discussion, the discourse on globalization and restructuring imposes certain biases through its frame of reference. It frames in only the business of technological restructuring: inventions, innovations, debates about increased productivity and increased economic activity. The larger social and moral questions are excluded. Thus, there's no debate about why the federal government should be spending billions of dollars every year to buy the latest in networking technology while laying off thousands of civil servants in the name of deficit cutting and fiscal restraint. There's no suggestion that the current high rates of unemployment and under-employment could be reduced (and could even have been avoided) if working people could negotiate technological restructuring — as a 1965 federal Commission of Inquiry strongly recommended (Menzies, 1996:24). As some case studies have demonstrated, people could negotiate to use information systems and other technologies to extend the scope of their work, rather than be replaced by these technologies. But that contingency, that technological-choice path, is ignored. And the loss or lack of social-justice policies requiring a democratic management of technological restructuring is hardly noticed.

The terms of reference mirror the depersonalization or alienation of people too. They emphasize only the economic aspects of people's existence as occupational data sets. Then they fragment that existence into such isolated issue topics as "two-tiered labour force" and "deskilling" and "skills for the new economy." Third, the official language of the discourse — the objectifying language of scientific rationality — bleeds the humanity out of what's happening to real people in real communities. Again, you can see the logic and values of prescriptive technology at work: depersonalizing experience, fragmenting it, disintegrating it out of the context of lived experience and reintegrating it as data in prescribed conceptual grids. Finally, only the people who speak that language — the designated experts, usually with credentials associated with academic disciplines — are considered as bona fide speakers (authorities) in the discourse.

If you're watching the video, notice how different the language is in the panel discussion. There is a sense of solidarity with the people caught at the punishing end of the very unequal power relationships associated with the new economy. Such discussions represent a new critical discourse, grounded in the lives of people in actual communities rather than in the technological framework that Grant worried would consume us all.

The panelists are: Pat Armstrong, director of and professor in the School of Canadian Studies at Carleton University and the author of several important books on technological restructuring; Theresa Johnson, Public Service Alliance of Canada's union coordinator on a government adjustment committee on government downsizing, and internationally respected for her analysis of telework; and Geoff Bickerton, a technological-change negotiator with the Canadian Union of Postal Workers and part of the union's national technological-change committee.

COMMENTARY ON SUPPLEMENTARY READINGS

1) Ursula Franklin, *The Real World of Technology*, Chapter 3.

Franklin explores a provocative idea in this chapter: namely that beneath the material and purely economic goals of technology, a more fundamental drive is toward control. If you think of McLuhan's metaphor that the medium is the message, she's suggesting that technology serves as a medium for the spread of control and management. Note in particular some of the following points:

* If you think of technology as a webwork, you can think of weaving it differently. Technology as system is a lot more rigid.

* Such technologies (prescriptive systems) require external management, control and planning.

* Some control is associated with the technology itself; it acts as an axis around which activity is organized. It shapes the task to be done.

* This control theme has to be understood in a nuanced way. It's not that everything is controlled, preordained and deterministic. Neither is everything possible, or depicted or perceived as possible or planned for as a possible option.

* Michel Foucault's research demonstrates the origins of a culture of control and self-control, in the invention of a new notion of discipline in 18th-century monastic communities. This philosophy fostered detailed hierarchial structures, drills, surveillance and record keeping.

* Labour discipline, resembling army discipline, pre-dated the machine-related disciplines of the industrial era.

* One of the earliest links between this new social discipline and state planning was in response to the Plague, where "total discipline" was imposed on a general population.

* Planning continued to thrive as an "activity closely associated with the exercise of control." In particular, this control served to inculcate certain social patterns, such as masses of disciplined factory labourers.

* Though it's not stated in the text, the Luddite movement arose in part because the state abolished a number of laws that had previously restricted the spread and use of mechanical looms. This gave a major boost of support to the interests associated with mechanization.

* The Luddites' struggle was largely over the theme of control, which an emerging alliance between the state and industrial capitalists was threatening to take away from ordinary working people, in the guise of the new technologies.

* The factory form of work organization imposed its ethic of remote and authoritarian control through the prescriptive division and fragmentation of labour and knowledge.

* Hydro power is a good illustration of how technologies become political and alternatives are squeezed out of the frame of political discussion.

* The state infrastructures of education, grant and contract giving plus regulation or non-regulation impose policy through the choice and development of technologies, such as nuclear technology, without any public discussion or a democratic vote. The current emphasis in education on skills development for the new economy teaches students computer literacy at the expense of moral literacy.

* State-supported discourses, from discussion to concrete actions and programs, fundamentally determine the rights of way of discussion and action. One way is by turning indivisible costs and benefits into divisible, individualized costs and benefits. One of the best examples is in transforming the indivisible cost of environmental pollution into a series of individualized solutions, such as treatments for asthma or for infertility. A battery of state- or corporate-supported "experts" tell us this is the problem, this is the solution.

2) Heather Menzies, three excerpts from *Whose Brave New World?*

Much of the material here repeats or elaborates on points already discussed in the video and the first section of this chapter. So I will simply highlight a few major points in each of the excerpts.

a) pp. 20-23

* The digital networks of the new economy are the new social and economic environment. They surround us, pulling together a host of previously separate activities associated with previously separate structures such as factory, home, bank, school, store.

* The networking phase of computerization is the most significant in terms of the paradigm shift that is occurring.

* The Information Highway, a generalized term for the network of intersecting networks, not just associated with the Internet but also with financial-information transactions and corporate information systems, marks this paradigm shift. It's lifting the corporate economy into cyberspace.

* It's creating a new form of corporate organization called the "virtual" corporation, or enterprise. The word "virtual" is used to signify an electronic essence or effect of a reality grounded in material terms. A corporation creates a virtual form of itself by sending files, data and even proprietary software via digital communication lines to a person's home or other outside locale.

* Virtual corporations might fulfil what Harold Innis called the bias of communication in the modern era. The bias toward fast media of communication has produced monopoly-scale structures

to support this. As these structures become invisible, so the monopoly scale of control becomes transparent.

* The state's role has been to support the private sector as the primary planners of the new economy.

b) pp. 65-69

* Technological restructuring in hospitals involves both management technologies (for instance, "patient care orders" and "value added" measures of activity) plus specific technological innovations gradually integrated into a hospital-wide system.

* There has been a consistent reorganization of work toward a core of full-time professionals and administrators and a periphery of part-time and contracted-out work.

* TQM has meant a narrowing of the meaning of work so that if it can't be computed, it won't be counted, and won't count. This has taken a heavy toll on people, particularly in almost punishing them for their own personal sense of commitment. As one nurse put it, "what happened to our judgement along the way?" The computer's judgement eclipsed it.

c) pp. 113-28

*The new phrase, "Traffic Operator Position System" (TOPS), in telephony symbolizes and illustrates the transformation of people into functioning parts of technological systems. They're also cut off from each other, through changing shifts and part-time positions and working in isolated work cubicles.

* Call centres and telework are major features of the new economy. Both epitomize the continuing trend toward fragmented, isolated work.

* Computer monitoring introduces the generalized features of a panopticon to workplaces. Foucault calls it a "super-panopticon."

* The dream of the original prison panopticon was that the people being watched would come to embrace the adherence to societal rules and regulations. A similar dream of getting people to identify with management's productivity and competitive goals might yet be realized as computer performance measures are accepted as a meaningful measure of work (and old ideas like giving personalized service to long-time customers are forgotten), as pay is based on meeting those performance measures, and as TQM cultural training actively solicits, and rewards, corporate identification.

* One research study actually used the thermostat servo-mechanism as its model in trying to design an ideal environment in which workers would respond well to preprogrammed cues, and discovered that it could work if it was made technically fair.

* Skills training, in the sense of people getting to do more and more challenging things with the new technologies, and gaining skills and knowledge useful to themselves, has been eclipsed by a new type of "cultural training." This training, which is useful to individuals only as long as they stay with the company, involves a lot of attitude adjustment. It's not coercive, but it's seductive in its invitation to join, to be part of the team, part of the corporate mission.

* The rhetoric is similar to the rhetoric of advertising, enticing identification with the product, with the cause. Individual identity is augmented by a new group identity.

* The new social Taylorism illustrates an earlier point about the depersonalization/fragmentation of work coming full circle, almost into reverse. As people become integrated into the new digital systems, they start to internalize the rules and dictates of the old Taylorism. They're encouraged to embrace that way of thinking, and to practice it themselves.

* The panoptical supervision of the systems in which people now find themselves working almost eliminates any choice in the matter. People "turn turtle." Like a turtle turned inside out, with its flesh exposed to direct poking and prodding, workers are exposed to being hard-wired, and programmed directly by the computer (see Chapter 6 for a fuller description of turning turtle).

* The examples provided illustrate the real dangers involved, and what this can do to human community.

* Although the "discourse" on technological restructuring only looks at this in individualized divisible terms, some important indivisible issues are at stake affecting our society and culture as a whole.

QUESTIONS FOR DISCUSSION

This unit concludes the second module of this course. It began with a discussion of industrial systems and their connection to empire building outside Canada and inside it as well. And it ended with the restructuring of industrial systems into post-industrial information networks serving the more generalized empire of global corporations.

Now, test your comprehension of the concepts discussed so far with the following questions:

1) Is the emerging global "information and knowledge" economy fundamentally different from the industrial economy or merely a scaled-up, speeded up (globalized) version of its biases and its rigidities? What are these biases and rigidities?
2) Are people becoming "servo-mechanisms" of technological systems under certain circumstances? If so, what does this entail?
3) How would you change the "discourse on technology" so that people's experiences, and related concerns, became central to it?

SOURCES AND FURTHER READINGS

Armstrong, Pat and Armstrong, Hugh, 1996. *Wasting Away: The Undermining of Canadian Health Care*. Toronto: Oxford University Press.

Coy, Peter, 1991. "How do you Build an Information Highway?" *Business Week* (September 16).

Freedman, Samuel, 1965. "Report of the Industrial Inquiry Commission on Canadian National Railways 'Run-Throughs.'" Ottawa: National Library.

Haraway, Donna J., 1991. *Simians, Cyborgs and Women: The Reinvention of Nature*. London: Free Association Books.

Industry Canada, 1994. *The Canadian Information Highway: Building Canada's Information and Communication Infrastructure*. Ottawa: Supply and Services.

Johnson, Theresa, 1993. *Go Home ... and Stay There? A PSAC Response to Telework in the Federal Public Service*. Ottawa: PSAC.

Langdon, Steven, 1975. *The Emergence of the Canadian Working Class Movement, 1845-75*. Toronto: New Hogtown Press.

Leiss, William, 1990. *Under Technology's Thumb*. Montreal: McGill-Queens Press.

McLuhan, Marshall, 1964. *Understanding Media: The Extensions of Man*. New York: Mentor.

Menzies, Heather, 1996. *Whose Brave New World? The Information Highway and the New Economy*. Toronto: Between the Lines.

Morissette, René and Sunter, Deborah, 1994. *What is Happening to Weekly Hours Worked in Canada?* Household Surveys, No. 65. Ottawa: Statistics Canada.

Morris, William, 1993. *Art and Society: Lectures and Essays by William Morris*, ed. Gary Zabel. Boston: George's Hill.

Sky, Laura, 1990. *Working Lean: Challenging Work Restructuring*. Film produced by Skyworks for the Canadian Auto Workers.

TRANSITION

CHAPTER 6

TECHNOLOGY, CULTURE AND DISCOURSE

OVERVIEW

This unit marks a turning point, where the discussion switches from the nuts and bolts of political economy to the softer bonds of culture and identity. The unit also encourages you to switch perspective a bit more along the lines of the preceding unit. For much of the first modules, we've looked at technology at some remove, historically and materially. This unit invites you to consider that you're living in a society that is increasingly defined by technological systems and technical ways of thinking, and how this shapes your view of the world and identity.

The unit begins with a selective review of Canadian paintings from what could be considered the industrial period of Canada. In the video, you'll see technology through Canadian artists' eyes, and note the differences in perspective, for instance, between commissioned and non-commissioned works. To bring this overview closer to the present, the video also includes a couple of excerpts from a computer-art exhibit held in Toronto in 1995. It then reviews the theme of technology in Canadian literature, noting the dominant perspectives in mainstream writing and the different perspectives from immigrant, native and some women writers.

These examples should help bring home the point that technology is considerably more than the TV in the corner and the source of jobs and economic growth. It also informs national, local and personal identity. Having done this, the unit then turns to the Canadian "discourse" on technology. Being close to the United States, Canadians benefit from the latest technologies from that technological heartland, and are almost swallowed up by them. However, Canada's traditions outside technology — traditional First Nations, rural, British and French institutions — indicate that we are not fully assimilated into the technological world order. There are many fine communication scholars whose work will be referred to in subsequent modules. Here, however, we'll concentrate on those who have addressed technology in general, and how it broadly affects society and identity. We'll explore the key ideas of George Grant, Harold Innis, Marshall McLuhan and Ursula Franklin. We'll look at why Grant has been called a "pessimist," and why Harold Innis and Ursula Franklin can best be seen as realists and pragmatists. We'll also challenge the popular, but perhaps too simplistic idea that McLuhan was an "optimist" on technology.

OBJECTIVES

At the end of this unit, you will be able to think more critically about how the technologies you depend on to make your way in the world also affect your sense of who you are and what you can become. You will have some sense, too, of Canadian thinking on technology, and the possibilities for human justice and freedom, human diversity and even personal spontaneity in a technological world.

You will be able to address, if not answer, the following questions:

1) Are people becoming servo-mechanisms of a technological dynamo?
2) Is there a dominant theme regarding technology in Canadian art and literature?
3) Who are some of the thinkers associated with the Canadian discourse on technology, and what is their perspective on technology?

A NEWSPAPER STORY IN 1995 reported a bizarre incident of someone taking over someone else's email account and starting to speak through that identity. Cynthia Sulaiman, moderator of an Islamic discussion group on the Internet, discovered that her password for her email account didn't work; worse still, postings were emerging from her account, written by someone else. Someone had effectively taken over her identity in order to misrepresent it and undermine her work. One posting told the 30,000 discussion-group subscribers that she was resigning, and asked members' forgiveness (Spender, 1995:254).

Such stories drive home the point that technology today is a powerful force shaping identity. It is as powerful and pervasive as the sea was to Newfoundland fisher-people, as the land has been to Canada's first peoples and, latterly to its farmers, and as iron-laced rock has been to immigrant mine workers, or the textile factory and kitchen has been for many women. Today, as people project their voices and identities through the Internet, the texts they write are the only way the virtual community out in cyberspace can identify them. Some people take on different identities, called signatures or SIGs, in different contexts, assuming a different gender, or voice or sexual orientation as they cross boundaries into this or that newsgroup or MUD (multi-user dungeon) group. Is there a coherent identity among the multiple personalities, and does that matter anymore?

By comparison, questioning technology's effect on identity was easier in the more grounded industrial phase of modernity. Art curator and teacher, Rosemary Donegan, put together a retrospective of Canadian artists' views on industrialism in 1987. In the catalogue accompanying the exhibit, she talked about the perceived centrality of industrial development to Canada's coming of age as a nation. And she discussed the dominant themes and images through which this industrialization was depicted in visual art.

On the one hand, she found a strong tradition of technological optimism, even hubris. Tellingly, though, this theme came through most in commissioned art, where artists worked as the hired painters of an official or prescribed vision, paid for either by the state or by business, and sometimes too by organized labour.

In the video, two paintings of the steel mills in Sydney, Nova Scotia, depict technology in slightly different tones. One is by Laura McLennan, a local woman artist, whose husband was a board member and shareholder of Dominion Steel. The daytime treatment, the watercolour techniques and the expansive water of the bay mute the steel plant to the point that it is "almost inconsequential"(Donegan, 1988:2). By contrast, the painting by Sir William Van

Horne, the putative "father" of the CPR, depicting the steel mills at night, clearly highlights the mill (see box).

"Van Horne's dramatic glorification of the blast furnaces is consistent with his own personal economic interests as a major shareholder and member of the Board, but also symbolized his personal belief in the industrial age as progressive, enterprising and profitable.... The [Dominion Iron and Steel Company] steel plant was a national industrial showpiece, and was seen as the new industrial ascendency of Nova Scotia." (Donegan, 1988:2)

The factory and the smokestack have been dominant icons of the industrial era, emblems with which people were encouraged to identify themselves as participating in a larger public and national identity. In Canada, however, the grain terminal was an equally if not more compelling image of the era. Partly this was because grain terminals and flour mills were prominent on the waterfronts of Montreal, Toronto and Vancouver. Partly, too, wheat symbolized a national economy, in that Prairie wheat was shipped by rail for processing in central Canada and Vancouver, before being exported.

"For the first time in history, the whole of transcontinental British North America was marching in unison through a period of unexampled prosperity.... It was a national success, in which all regions participated, which linked all regions for the first time in a common material interest based on the vast expansion of the wheat-producing west." (Creighton, 1962:393-94)

Canada chose to represent itself by a grain elevator at the 1937 International Exhibition in Paris, with a design that won a prize for its bold modernity. Inside the Mining Building at the exhibition, Charles Comfort's "The Romance of Nickel" was equally modern in its heroic scale and stripped-down simplicity. Comfort, who began work as a commercial artist illustrating for Eaton's catalogues, was commissioned by Inco to do the 10 by 20-foot mural.

Romance of Nickel, by Charles Comfort. (Mrs. Irene Comfort)

By contrast, Montreal artist, Adrien Hébert, depicts a man dwarfed by the terminal architecture in the port of Montreal. Marion Scott, another Montreal artist, evokes a similar sense of the menace of large-scale technology in "Cement." Donegan noted that such paintings were "part of a larger discussion among artists and intellectuals of urban and industrial alienation."

At an international exhibit of computer art, called *Press Enter*, held in Toronto's Power Plant gallery in 1995, curator Louise Dompierre set out to create a space where artists could explore the "soft future" of the computer age, the "mental marriage to technology" — a technology that "does not act, it evokes," she wrote in the catalogue (Dompierre, 1995:17). With the possible exception of Québécois artist, Luc Courchesne's optimistic "Family Portrait: Encounter with a Virtual Society," the Canadian artists were ambivalent about this future of evoked virtual identities.

David Rokeby's "Silicon Remembers Carbon" is a participative exhibit involving a projected image of water on a large shallow silicon/sandbox in a darkened room. As viewers walk around the box, shadows suddenly appear in the sandbox. They seem to be the viewers' shadow, but are not. The effect is confusing. As Rokeby explains in the video, the idea is to get people to think twice. As we project ourselves into constructed spaces, the selves we think we see aren't necessarily our own reflections/projections.

Christine Davis' "Le dictionnaire des inquisiteurs (tombeau)" invites the viewer to consider how the truths and realities through which we live our lives are composed through layers of technological constructions; here, words inscribed by laser beam onto the surface of used contact lenses (an early prosthetic device) encased in a plexiglass tomb.

CANADIAN LITERATURE Margaret Atwood dared to sum up the dominant theme in Canadian literature in the one-word title of her 1972 essay, *Survival*. And certainly this might have summed up the European newcomers, daunted by the harsh landscape they encountered. The sense of geography comes through clearly in some of the main texts and most commonly known writers of pan-Canadian history, although with a notable difference of perspective by First Nations' writers (see box).

> "Yet geography has offered Canada much as well. This giant land has held rich rewards for those ready to meet its challenge." (Careless, 1970:3)
>
> "The history of Canada must begin as it were pre-natally. The country of today was not born until generations of Europeans had tramped across the surface of the New World, had fought each other in its fastnesses, had given themselves in toil against the wilderness....These men ... brought to birth Canada, child of European civilization and the American wilderness." (Lower, 1964:1)
>
> "Ouvrons un atlas.... Première impression, l'immensité. Mais la nature est moins généreuse que le territoire est vaste." (Lacour-Gayet, 1966:22)
>
> "Canada, it used to be said by non-Indians with more or less conviction, is a country of much geography and little history. The ethnocentricity of that position at first puzzled and even confused Amerindians, but it has lately begun to anger them." (Dickason, 1992:11)

Technology was the means of conquering and domesticating the land, and this became a prominent image in Canadian literature, except in Quebec where the pastoral theme — not space, but time and the preservation of language, culture and religion — predominated until the postwar period.

E.J. Pratt's 1952 epic poem, *Towards the Last Spike*, epitomizes the dominance-through-technology theme, with its heroic, even mythic imagery. Pratt likens Donald Smith to a Moses, and describes the workers as standardized units in a vast production machine that triumphs over nature.

Technological optimism might have predominated in the cultural mainstream where poets like Pratt held celebrity status. Outside it, however, more ambivalent and negative views have prevailed. Examples include Archibald Lampman's 1888 "The Railway Station," John Flood's *The Land they Occupied* (1976) and Margaret Avison's "Perspective," (1980) (see box).

> Do you not miss the impact of that fierce
> Raw boulder five miles off? You are not pierced
> By that great spear of grass on the horizon?
> You are not smitten with the shock
> Of that great thundering sky? (Avison in Jones, 1987:43)

Frederick Philip Grove grappled with the mastering power and appeal of technology, as well as its power to master (see box).

> "[I]n reality, the pace forces him to be constantly on the watch; it isn't that he becomes a machine; that would be tolerable if undesirable. What he becomes is the slave of a machine ..." (Grove, 1967:193)

The anti-technology theme in Canadian literature has been closely aligned to anti-Americanism and anti-modernism. Margaret Atwood's *Surfacing* is a curious blend of this combination played out in a poetic odyssey of personal growth. The protagonist grapples with technology, not just on the large-scale terms of empire, but personally in terms of her having used the technology of abortion. By coming to terms with what she denied within herself in making this choice, she finds the courage to reenter the technological world but on her own terms. Atwood's later novel, *The Handmaid's Tale*, is more deeply pessimistic.

There is also the literature produced by immigrant and ethnic minority writers, and Canada's first peoples. Here, the view of technology tends to be pessimistic, but it's not anti-technology as such. Technology is a given here, the terrain in which people struggle to survive. It's a socially constructed terrain. It's not technology as abstraction, but as experience, and particularly the experience of unequal relations of power.

> "It is 1930. The cut of the shovel into clay is all Patrick sees digging into the brown slippery darkness. He feels the whole continent in front of him. They dig underneath one of the largest lakes in North America beside a hissing lamp, racing with the speed of their shadows.... All morning they slip in the wet clay unable to stand properly, pissing where they work, eating where someone else left shit." (Ondaatje, 1987:105)

In Michael Ondaatje's *In the Skin of a Lion*, the workers have no choice. If they want to eat, they have to work on the big infrastructure projects such as the Toronto waterworks (see box).

These same three themes, technological optimism, technological pessimism and an often equally pessimistic realism, can be found in the Canadian discourse on technology.

THE CANADIAN DISCOURSE ON TECHNOLOGY Cultural critic, Arthur Kroker, argued in his 1985 book, *Technology and the Canadian Mind*, that there is a distinctly Canadian discourse on technology. Canadians have a unique perspective on modern technology because we are neither fully part of the American technological empire nor fully outside it. We're "midway between privilege and dependency," both insiders on technology and outsiders too. We're also a living experiment on whether it is possible to live critically within the dynamo of a fully realized technological society.

GEORGE GRANT George Grant was a deeply religious Conservative philosopher with United Empire Loyalist roots. Over a long career teaching religion and philosophy at two Canadian universities, Grant developed a sustained critique of modern liberal technology in books and articles, which enjoyed considerable popular attention. Essentially, he enlarged a political analysis of colonization and empire into a broadly philosophical one. He shifted from considering the colonization of countries to the colonization of consciousness: from the conquering of external material space through commercialism to conquering internal mental space through the empire of technique. To use the Innis differentiation, Grant's bias was toward the spiritual concerns of time: time as tradition, conservation and permanence. He saw these traditions as threatened both by the rise of American liberalism and the triumph of technical rationality as the dominant approach to thinking in virtually every aspect of public life.

Where in his earliest writings, he castigated the manifest destiny of American imperialism, in his later writings, he critiqued the manifest destiny of technological mastery and self-mastery.

Go back and reread the section in Unit 3 dealing with the core themes of European modern thought, which informed the approaches to science and technology associated with the European newcomers to Canada. Grant's is a critique of how these values converged into a purely technological utilitarianism. Where religion used to provide a grounding place of values outside that of technological mastery and domination, all that remains now, he argued, is "the self-propelling will to technology." What's worse, it's equated with "the liberation of mankind." But if anyone tries to define liberty in terms other than those conforming to technological expansionism, he argues, they can do so only in the confines of their private lives. He argued that the institutions associated with public civic society — notably the church and the university — had succumbed to the rule of practical liberalism and technical rationality.

> "The moral discourse of 'values' and 'freedoms' is not independent of the will to technology, but a language fashioned in the same forge together with the will to technology." (Grant, 1969:32)

Grant also argued that the effect of being enclosed in the empire of technology is to be colonized by a mind set where the technical values of speed and productivity are treated as ends in themselves. The results of this assimilation are dependency in the deepest possible sense. People become dependent on this way of thinking for defining the meaning of their existence. Hence Grant's image of people reduced to servo-mechanisms of the technological dynamo, ceaselessly turning over new products, either as producers or consumers, but without knowing whether this has meaning beyond a wage or a price tag.

> "Therefore as our liberal horizons fade in the winter of nihilism, and as the dominating amongst us see themselves within no horizon except their own creating of the world, the pure will to technology (whether personal or public) more and more gives sole content to that creating.... We now move toward the position where technological progress becomes itself the sole context within which all that is other to it must attempt to be present." (Grant, 1969:40)

For Grant, such a state of existence isn't freedom, but tyranny — in the form predicted by Hegel when he interpreted the decline of theism, or the belief in a larger being and purpose, as signalling the move toward a universal and homogenous state.

Grant offered a sweeping indictment of modern technological society. But it had two major flaws. First, Grant considered that public agency (the ability to act and make changes) in society rested solely with the dominant institutions and their leaders. Second, he didn't check out his abstract arguments with the people for whom he was speaking in making them. For example, he was a vehement anti-abortionist, depicting women as servo-mechanisms of the "right" and the "freedom" to have abortions. Yet he never checked this assertion against women's actual experience, thoughts and feelings.

Harold Innis and Ursula Franklin offer a useful contrast to these broad philosophical statements.

HAROLD INNIS Innis grew up on a farm in western Ontario, boarded in town through high school, then went to Toronto and eventually to Chicago for university. His mother's hopes that he become a minister were lost in the prolonged agony of the trenches of World War I. Innis came home with photos he'd taken, bearing witness. He spent much of the rest of his life in that sort of detailed witnessing: researching the present and the past, trying to understand the forces that could come together in such deterministic acts of human destruction, so that others might learn how to offset them.

While Grant viewed technology in almost purely philosophical terms, or as an embodiment of certain philosophical ideas, Innis saw it in much more material terms. Like Grant, he was searching for

Harold Innis. University of Toronto Archives

the inner ideas at work within technology. But he picked his way through the nitty-gritty of technology's social and physical constructs to find these ideas. He believed in field research to avoid becoming hostage to rigid theoretical assumptions.

In his early work, documenting the history of the cod fishery, the fur trade and the CPR, Innis uncovered the contradictions in the conventional wisdom, inherited from British schools of economic thought, that exporting staples to a more developed country (Britain) was a natural stepping-stone to development in a new country. By reinterpreting staples exports from the viewpoint of Canada, as a stepping-stone into dependency and underdevelopment, Innis laid the groundwork for a distinctly Canadian-centred analysis of Canada's economic development, and earned the epithet of "marginal man"; that is, someone taking the view from the margin, and not automatically identifying with the centre of conventional wisdom.

These studies also alerted him to the power of transportation and communication technologies in shaping the larger patterns of civilizations. His most enduring legacy is in his insights here, such as the ***bias of communication***. By this, he meant that every medium of communication embodied a particular values bias. Sometimes this was inherent in the medium itself; for instance, the oral medium of conversation and dialogue is inherently democratic as no special equipment or skills are needed. More often, though, the bias is built into the material and social structures associated with a medium; for example, books and the organization of work in a publishing house.

In studying the rise and fall of different civilizations, Innis found a pattern of some media being biased toward the sacred values of time, while others were geared to the more secular values of space. Moreover, Innis found that discovering these biases was akin to discovering the core biases of the civilization itself. For instance, societies that used stone tablets as a medium of communication, such as Moses and the Ten Commandments, tended to be time-biased societies, concerned with permanence and eternity, not material gain, fashion turnover and spatial expansion. On the other hand, Egyptian papyrus, which was adopted by the Greeks and also the Romans, was easy to write on and easy to transport, which suited the space-conquering empire builders.

The strength of Innis' analysis was in his grasp of the reciprocal relation between the bias of communication and the bias of the society in which this media was employed. And so today, both the physical properties of electronic media (non-material and instantly transportable) and the global commercial corporations associated with its use are important clues to the continuing bias of space in the post-modern era.

Innis' work is also important for its materialist understanding of communication technology. He understood how large-scale systems of communication could become rigid. He could appreciate how the rigidity of unused capacity in media would bias it toward quantity over quality, and toward the mass audience over the particular local audience. He could also predict how the rigidity of fixed costs could create structural monopolies in media ownership (see Unit 8). He saw parallels between material monopolies such as the Hudson's Bay Company and the CPR and monopolies of knowledge and perception (see Unit 9). He even saw a direct connection between large-scale resource extraction (pulp and paper), large-scale transportation and the rise of mass-circulation newspapers (see Unit 7). Innis also predicted that the rigidities that made these various systems unstable would also make societies unstable.

Above all, Innis was interested in offsetting that instability. His solution lay not in the political arena of ideologies, but in the pragmatic arena of institutions. He also championed the oral tradition both as a way to break monopolies of knowledge associated with text-bound truths and theories, and as a way to know one's self. Self-knowledge, not just personal self-knowledge but critical knowledge of one's culture, was central to Innis' "plea for time," and attainable through the dialogue of the seminar class in university. He believed that a culture's health depended on people's ability to think for themselves, and to resist the rigidities of group-think. He also believed in freedom in the old Whig tradition as something cultivated, with an attendant sense of social responsibility, through public institutions such as universities.

URSULA FRANKLIN Ursula Franklin grew up in a cultured German home, with an art historian as mother and an engineer/archaeologist as a father. Coming of age as Hitler was coming to power, she was attracted to physics as a field of study at the Technical University of Berlin, in part because here were truths of nature which, as she put it in a documentary, even the Nazi propaganda machine couldn't bend. She and her family were prisoners in a forced-labour camp during the war. Afterward, she was one of the first post-war refugees to enter Canada. She spent her career teaching physics and pioneering a new interdisciplinary science, the science of ancient materials. She had other, less formal careers as well: as a deeply committed peace activist, feminist, environmentalist and with a particular interest in citizen-based civic planning.

I have known her for some 15 years; she has been both a mentor and a friend. So it's a particular pleasure to include her here in this course.

Like Innis, Franklin views technology as a social construct involving human choice and embodying chosen values. Like Innis, too, she sees technology becoming deterministic in its effects once a particular design has been implemented. Franklin's analysis takes in both the material aspects of technology and the non-material aspects associated with planning and discipline. Hence, Franklin describes contemporary technological society as a "culture of compliance" mediated by prescriptive technological systems.

The realism and pragmatism of Innis are also apparent in Franklin, as is the pessimism. But then the differences emerge.

Unlike Innis, Franklin clearly names the military axis around which much of contemporary technological practice turns. Military research and development has been the site for a formidable partnership between government and industry. Furthermore, Franklin argues, the arms-production industry serves as an infrastructure "for the advancement of technology." This not only promotes what her colleague, Anatol Rapaport, calls the "technological imperative," the constant search for technological solutions to societal needs and problems. It also perpetuates "the need for a credible long-term enemy," if not outside one's country, then within it.

While Innis has been criticized at times for concentrating too much on the material side of technological systems, Franklin emphasizes the social dimensions. This is evident in the stress she lays on planning, on the disciplining power of bureaucratic rules and on "constructed realities" of prescriptive knowledge systems, which she likens to an "occupation force of immense power" (Franklin, 1990:44).

Franklin is also a feminist, and uses women's perspectives, women's experiences and women's voices throughout her critique of technology. In a sense, this exacerbates her pessimism, as she is more keenly aware of the domination-and-control ethic underlying prescriptive technological practice. At the same time, though, it gives her reason to hope. Positioning herself with women who are considered "outside" and "on the margins of" technology, she attests to the technological agency apparent in women's experience as technological practitioners. Identifying with this perspective, she uses it to champion a more participatory, rather than a pre-planned technological practice. For her, women's often very different approaches to life — coping rather than planning, for example — suggest ways of weaving "the web of our technology" differently. She also believes that this other web can only be woven if the discourse on technology can itself be freed from its culture of compliance to prescriptive constructed realities engineered by experts. In other words, people who speak the vernacular language of experienced reality should be at the centre of defining the public agenda on technology. Applying this conviction herself, Franklin dots her text with references to everyday life, including the poem about "Another Silly Typing Error." She also writes in simple, accessible language, another gesture of solidarity with the people whose agency she would champion in redesigning/redefining technology as if people mattered.

MARSHALL MCLUHAN The son of an encyclopedia salesman and a cultured expert on elocution, Edmonton-born Marshall McLuhan studied English at Cambridge, learning to adapt the practice of literary criticism to a generalized approach to studying contemporary media environments (Marchand, 1989). In the process, he became both social critic and an artist himself.

Many of his aphorisms seem inspired by that role. Playing the artist, he used words to create an "anti-environment," a shift of perspective that allowed people to see more readily the forest for the trees in developments around them.

Consider his aphorism: "In the Information Age, man lives not by bread alone, but by slogans also" (McLuhan, 1970:42).

Here, McLuhan shifts the ground of common knowledge, where the Biblical reference to bread is followed by a reference to faith. Suddenly, we must contemplate the idea that modern faith is housed in advertising agencies.

Then there's McLuhan's most famous aphorism: "the medium is the message." This means that the structures of communication strongly determine the content of communication and the culture that transpires as a result. The structures include the physical medium itself plus the social relations and organizational structures. While Innis focused on the material and organizational structures, McLuhan concentrated more on the physiological effects.

This focus also suited McLuhan's rhetorical style. Canadian author and former McLuhan student, Bruce Powe, called it the "put-on" which he translated to mean "personality as probe." McLuhan's style was intensely oral and aural, emulating what Judith Stamps describes as his "negative dialect" response to a homogenizing modernity associated with print and the mass media (Stamps, 1995:127-38). He deliberately juxtaposed images, dangled sentence fragments, refused the conventions of linear thought and rational exposition. Through the structures of his own personal style of communication, he attempted to create an acoustic environment that his listeners (and readers) could enter. He prepared the ground for people to engage their own powers of critical perception, and apply it to becoming critically aware of the biases permeating modern secular society. In a sense, he styled himself as the nymph, Echo, waking people out of their hypnotic devotion to technology.

> "In the '80s there will be a general awareness that the technology game is out of control, and that perhaps man was not intended to live at the speed of light.... It might even be said that at the speed of light man has neither goals, objectives nor private identity. He is an item in the data bank — software only, easily forgotten — and deeply resentful." (McLuhan, 1980:32)

McLuhan, therefore, was far from being the optimist he's popularly depicted as. He described himself as a Catholic humanist, whose job, he felt was "to build bridges between the arts and society today." The traditions associated with the arts, embodying their reverence for human memory, and for resonance of sensory experience, were his grounding place against the constantly changing figures of modern technology.

COMMENTARY ON SUPPLEMENTARY READINGS

1) George Grant, "In Defence of North America," in *Technology and Empire*.

Mostly, this reading is intended to give you a sense of George Grant's ideas and personality first hand. But note the following points:

* The unchosen fate of being Canadian includes having been caught up in the affairs of empires — French, British, American.

* Our participation in the American empire goes beyond the political and economic to include an underlying faith in progress through technique which underlies the power of this empire.

* This faith is a blend of Protestantism plus the secular influences of material science and a moral science of individualism, originating with Machievelli and domesticated by English liberals.

* Modern liberalism equates the homogenizing power of technology with the achievement of human "excellence," and expresses this as individual material gain.

* The modern world view creates a moral tension between allegiance to idealized technological/imperial projects and allegiance to one's particular community and self. The love of one's own is the stepping-stone to a larger love of, and allegiance to, the public good.

* This is at odds with the modern "religion of progress" and its faith that the conquest of human and non-human nature gives meaning to everything.

* Behind the crumbling faith in Canadian nationalism is a larger existential question: what is worth doing in this barren twilight of nihilism when there's no meaning left but technological progress for the sake of technological progress?

2) Harold Innis, "A Plea for Time," in *The Bias of Communication*.

* Innis begins by announcing that the modern era is marked by a disappearance of an interest in time and all that it has traditionally stood for: experience, memory, continuity, permanence, eternity.

* Instead, time has been systematically transformed by the space bias. Social time has lost its religious roots, and become linear, historical and increasingly contractual. It's no longer round like the seasonal cycles. Now it's square, with deadlines.

* But a stable society depends on a balance between space and time. And so, the bias of space in the Roman empire, applied through the medium of papyrus, was offset by the use of parchment for religious texts. In turn, the monopoly of the church, with its control over parchment texts, almost invited the rise of a new medium — paper and the printing press, through which the church's monopoly in society was broken.

3) Ursula Franklin, Chapter 6, *The Real World of Technology.*

Franklin sums up her lecture series with what is needed if "the real world of technology" is to become "a globally liveable habitat" instead of a panoptical fortress.

* Technological practice must become participatory rather than expert driven.

* The focus of planning must change from "maximizing gain" to a coping strategy of "minimizing disaster."

* Just as a good shoemaker must understand feet, so technological practice must understand and respect human needs and diversity.

* We are the real world of technology.

* "Redemptive" technological practice begins with a new critical discourse on technology, using language to clarify rather than mystify values and choices. For example, asking "whose" benefits and costs instead of "what" benefits and costs can highlight the contradictions associated with the emerging global digital economy.

* This discourse must be centred in action as well as words, with the idea that technology is what people do in the present moment.

* Redemptive technological practice could range from safely dismantling technologies (such as nuclear) that do not pass the people-centred approval process, to sponsoring technological projects that meet real human needs.

4) Marshall McLuhan, Introduction, *Understanding Media.*

This short excerpt from McLuhan's delightfully provocative book on the "extensions of man" serves as a good introduction both to McLuhan's style and his sometimes brilliant thoughts.

* His idea that the fragmented world of mechanized type is "imploding" with the universal connectivity of electronic communication is central to his ideas about a new age of tribal-like cultural integration in the "global village."

* This era marks the final "extension" of humankind: the simulated extension of human consciousness through the wires and satellite connections of digital communication.

* This implies a loss of privacy, and a vulnerability to being manipulated — e.g., by advertisers.

* Individual perspective is irrevocably changed. With inter-connecting media and speed-up, action and reaction merge. The result is that people live "mythically and integrally," in the total sensory experience of fast-flowing sounds and images from everywhere all at once.

* But this creates anxiety because people participate without being able to think this through for themselves, to be critically aware of the terms on which they're participating.

* A private point of view is obsolete, a product of the literary rationality associated with the editorial chair. The chair has been replaced by the psychiatrist's couch, the repository of feelings.

QUESTIONS FOR DISCUSSION

1) How are Harold Innis and Ursula Franklin similar in their analysis of technology, and how are they different?
2) How are George Grant and Marshall McLuhan similar, and how do they differ in their views?
3) What are some of the critical differences in art, literature and philosophical discussions, between technological optimism, technological pessimism and technological realism?

SOURCES AND FURTHER READINGS

Atwood, Margaret, 1972. *Survival*. Toronto: Anansi Press.

Careless, J.M.S., 1970. *Canada: A Story of Challenge*. Toronto: Macmillan.

Creighton, Donald, 1962. *Dominion of the North: A History of Canada*. Toronto: Macmillan.

Dickason, Olive Patricia, 1996. *Canada's First Nations: A History of Founding Peoples from Earliest Times*. Toronto: Oxford University Press.

Dompierre, Louise, 1995. *Press Enter: Between Seduction and Disbelief*. Toronto: The Power Plant — Contemporary Art Gallery.

Donegan, Rosemary, 1988. *Industrial Images/Images Industrielles*. Hamilton: The Art Gallery of Hamilton.

Grant, George, 1969. *Technology and Empire: Perspectives on North America*. Toronto: Anansi Press.

Grove, Frederick Philip, 1967. *The Master of the Mill*. Toronto: McClelland and Stewart.

Innis, Harold, 1984. *The Bias of Communication*. Toronto: University of Toronto Press.

Jones, Douglas, 1987. "Steel Syntax: The Railroad as Symbol in Canadian Poetry," in *Symbols in Life and Art*. Montreal: McGill-Queen's University Press.

Kroker, Arthur, 1985. *Technology and the Canadian Mind: Innis/McLuhan/Grant*. Montreal: New World Perspectives.

Lacour-Gayet, Robert, 1966. *Histoire du Canada*. Montreal: Fayard.

Lower, Arthur, 1964. *Colony to Nation: A History of Canada*. Toronto: Longmans.

Marchand, Philip, 1989. *Marshall McLuhan: The Medium and the Messenger*. New York: Ticknor and Fields.

McLuhan, Marshall, 1970. *Culture is Our Business*. New York: McGraw-Hill.

McLuhan, Marshall, 1980. "Living at the Speed of Light," *Maclean's* (January 7).

McLuhan, Marshall, 1996. *Understanding Media: The Extensions of Man*. Boston: MIT Press.

Ondaatje, Michael, 1987. *In the Skin of a Lion*. Toronto: McClelland and Stewart.

Spender, Dale, 1995. *Nattering on the Net: Women, Power and Cyberspace*. Toronto: Garamond Press.

Stamp, Judith, 1995. *Unthinking Modernity: Innis, McLuhan and the Frankfurt School*. Montreal: McGill-Queen's University Press.

MODULE III

COMMUNICATION, CULTURE AND IDENTITY

This module moves you closer to the global village of the title. It prepares the ground for critically assessing the emerging "village" of instant global communications by examining how its constituent media systems, everything from print to cable television, themselves came into being. And it cultivates the idea that the media environment in which we live fundamentally shapes our sense of who we are and what we dream of becoming.

This module also shifts the discussion from the structures of political economy, to the structures that shape culture and identity. It makes the connections between how we communicate and how we know ourselves, and frame our identity through different media of communication. It does this with a continuing emphasis on technology as a social construct. It takes everything you've learned about technology as tool, system and infrastructures of national and international economies, and applies this to studying the media of culture. This integrated perspective is particularly relevant today as the two types of structures (economic and cultural) are becoming indistinguishable from each other.

Chapter 7 is an important starting point because it introduces the first of the mass media that are the norm of public communication today. It shows how print technology developed from the simple tool of the printing press to the large-scale systems of mass-circulation newspapers. It also identifies some of the critical choices made along the way. It begins with the shift from oral to written communication, when communication is separated from the human body and increasingly abstracted and scaled up in space and time.

Chapter 8 provides a short history of radio, television and film. In the briefest of overviews, it identifies the key institutional players, including the state, and the critical choice paths and related values pursued in each of these media developments. It also looks at the alternative models of media development and what impact they have had on public and popular culture, especially on what is defined as the mainstream, or culture of the centre.

Chapter 9 concentrates on the effects of these media structures on what we know, how we know, plus the shared knowledge base that constitutes a culture. It considers how people become dependent on outside authorities, not because these experts have all the answers but because people have come to expect experts to have better knowledge, insight and perspective than non-experts. It also ties this back to world view, discussed in Unit 3. It considers how structures of communication and world views are reciprocally related, or how they reinforce each other.

OBJECTIVES

At the end of this module, you will know how to critically analyze today's mass media as rigid systems of information/knowledge production and equally rigid systems of information distribution. You will also understand the connection between mass audiences and mass culture. But equally you will understand the connection between diverse local cultures and the different models of media communication they employ, often in the margins of the mainstream. You will also have some important thinking tools for talking about cyberspace, the information society and the global village beyond the level of technical gadgets; at the level of organizational structures, social relationships and underlying values.

CHAPTER 7

THE INDUSTRIALIZATION OF KNOWING

OVERVIEW

This chapter looks at the difference between the knowledge contained in personal conversation and the knowledge imparted through the official channels of media communication. It dissects what happens when knowledge is separated from the direct telling of human experience and is channelled instead through written and printed texts. Scale emerges as an important factor here. As Unit 4 made clear, scale, particularly the scale-up of transportation, was key to the spread of an industrial model of economic development. Similarly with communication, knowledge and culture. Scale-up of communication has been a key factor in the industrialization of knowing; that is, its transformation into the production and consumption of knowledge.

This unit will introduce you to different theoretical approaches to the study of communication. The ***transmission*** school concentrates on media as neutral, structural conveyances, and treats content as something quite separate. The ***semiotics*** school treats content largely in isolation from the structures, or carriers. It focuses on the messages being sent, and the people on the receiving end of those messages. This unit will blend the two approaches in a ***materialist*** or social-context approach to communication. It will pay attention to the organizational structures involved, and the vested interests associated with them. It will also pay attention to scale, and the money required to achieve the scale of, say, mass-circulation newspapers and newspaper chains. Finally, it will note the messages conveyed through these communication structures, and how the structures of communication strongly influence what those messages are.

Applying McLuhan's aphorism "the medium is the message," it will spell out some of the "messages" built into the structures and organizational practices of today's media systems, including textbook publishers. It will then apply some of these lessons to the larger medium of our cultural milieu and explore the connection between communication media and what cultural themes can flourish, or not, through them.

OBJECTIVES

At the end of this unit, you should be able to answer the following questions:

1) What were the critical factors that influenced the rise of modern mass print media?
2) What other choice paths were there?
3) What are the key differences between oral and written communication?
4) Which of these differences make it easier to turn text-based knowing into an industrial model of mass production and consumption?

STUDYING THE SOCIAL CONTEXT of communication is a way to study both the institutional powers associated with the "political economy of communication" and the agency of people on the receiving end, which is covered more in "cultural studies." It helps us to resist seeing media structures as too deterministic, and people on the receiving end as purely passive. It also helps us avoid overstating the agency of people as readers, listeners and viewers of communication media. The social-context approach reveals a dialectic of relative power and, in some cases, stark imbalances of power, which have profound consequences for public knowledge and cultural stability.

> "We can perhaps assume that the use of a medium of communication over a long period will to some extent determine the character of knowledge to be communicated and suggest that its pervasive influence will eventually create a civilization in which life and flexibility will become exceedingly difficult to maintain." (Innis, 1984:34)

ORAL COMMUNICATION Oral communication can certainly be controlled. The rules governing who can speak the word of God in church, or the arcane rules recognizing, or not, Members of Parliament, during Question Period are ample proof of this. However, for anyone born with the ability to speak, that natural ability is hard to control. There are no special skills involved, no extra technologies are required to communicate in the oral tradition. So it lends itself to ***holistic*** cultural practice; that is, the open, spontaneous communication of personal conversation, seminar class discussion or political debate. Participants control the communication process, and the knowledge produced emerges from their autonomous speech. Being an organic form of communication, it is inherently flexible too. As Innis has noted, this tends to give oral cultures a wonderful vitality.

Oral communication is, therefore, more inherently democratic than printed communication, simply because there are few if any barriers to inclusive participation. ***Reciprocity***, one of the virtues on Ursula Franklin's list of design features for a people-centred technological world order, is also easier to maintain. In the electronic discussions in this course, you have the chance to say "ya, but." You can challenge an idea that has been presented in the text or video, and you can offer your own knowledge and perspective. When I taught this course entirely in an open seminar format, I incorporated what I'd learned from students' comments into what I said in the next year's seminar on this or that topic. The current course format makes this harder to do. This text is fixed and rigid, and so is the video. I could change these every year, but it is expensive, which makes it rigid. It's more costly than simply changing the words coming out of my mouth, or changing what I post in an electronic discussion group, and others have to approve this additional cost.

Electronic discussions are no substitute for face-to-face oral communication either. With the seminar class, you have fully embodied communication. There's the human voice itself, and all its dramatic gestures. You also have hand gestures and other body language, plus eye contact that says, "Yes! I'm listening, I care, and am moved or persuaded, or not." The sense of collegiality and community in electronic discussion groups is similar to the community that emerges in face-to-face seminar classes. But it's definitely not the same. We'll talk about this more in Unit 10 as we explore the growing culture of virtual communities and virtual reality. On the one hand, they are permitting the expression of some voices and realities that have been silenced or stigmatized in mainstream society; on the other, they are displacing many grounded realities associated with real geographic communities.

The medium is the message.

Harold Innis. University of Toronto Archives

FROM ORAL TO WRITTEN TO PRINT The move from oral to written communication marked a dramatic distancing of communication from the human body. It was a radical act of disembodiment and abstraction. Living words became inert objects on a page. Communication was no longer a continuous process linking speaker and receiver. It became discontinuous, with time and space widening the gap between them. Letters were sent across vast distances. They were read days or even years after they had been written.

The written word was, to McLuhan, an extension of the tongue and the mind. But since it was disembodied, it also raised the question: an extension of whose tongue and whose mind? With the written word, communication became increasingly organized. The specialized skills involved in writing lent themselves to a specialized division of labour. In the copying of religious texts onto parchment in monasteries across Medieval Europe, a distinct production model emerged. Certain monks, designated as scribes, did the copying; others, the illuminating. And everything they wrote was strictly prescribed within the hierarchy of the church and its councils of orthodoxy. In fact, the word orthodox, which means adhering to the accepted or traditional faith, is derived from the ancient Greek for "correct" (*orthos*) and "opinion" and "thinking" (*doxa* and *dokein*). Through its monopoly over copying, and copyists, the church effectively controlled the knowledge that was communicated as the official knowledge, or orthodoxy, of the day.

Despite these rigidities, the written alphabet retained some flexibility. Innis has noted that the Phoenician traders developed a script with 22 consonants to mimic the sounds of any of the languages they encountered in their travels. The legacy of this is the enduring idea of phonetical spelling, which has flourished in post-modern literature, affirming the particulars of local and racial vernaculars. But the standardizing, homogenizing effects of an abstract written alphabet were substantial, especially after writing entered the age of mechanical reproduction.

MECHANICAL REPRODUCTION It's important not to overemphasize material technologies over social, organizational ones. Still, the invention of mechanical presses, and particularly their scale-up for multiple copying, was in fact a vital factor in the development of standardized, homogenized mass communication. The earlier discussion about the phases of technological development (see Unit 2) helps too in distinguishing between the invention of the printing press and its more mature state in the form of integrated printing and distribution systems. It's worth reviewing the steps involved in that development.

One of the enabling steps was the invention of a new form of cheap paper, made from wood pulp as opposed to rags. This low-cost base for the media instantly opened it up for mass production and mass circulation because the cost per unit could be kept low enough that many people could afford it, not just the wealthy few. The new pulp for paper dropped the price of newsprint by nearly 800 percent, from 8.5 cents a pound to 1.5 cents a pound (Innis, 1949:6).

Certainly, the various interest groups that had broken the copyists monopoly on the written word by using the printing press instead could have continued using the small hand-operated presses. The early forms of publishing, associated with translations of the Gospels to the vernacular, the single broadsheet news and short pamphlet-like publications (such as Thomas Paine's *The Rights of Man*, published in the 1790s) could have continued. There was no inherent momentum toward mass-circulation publishing featuring a few sources of communication and multiple mass receivers. However, the commercial interests associated with the emerging industrial economy backed key technological developments which would first create a mass-production model of print communication, and then consolidate it as dominant.

The New York *Herald*'s double supplement press with a capacity of 24,000 copies of 12 pages each was surpassed by a quadruple press installed by its rival, the New York *World*, with a capacity of

48,000 copies of 8 pages each, and then again by an octuple press with a capacity of 96,000 copies of 8 pages per hour. All this technological one-upmanship happened within a few years. Understandably, it cost a lot.

To make this pay off financially, newspapers had to enlarge their circulation. To do this, publishers introduced innovations to give newspapers a mass-market appeal. They improved techniques for reproducing illustrations, and increased the number of these. By 1900, nearly all daily newspapers in the US were illustrated. They also introduced the cartoon, making newspapers something people could consume, as entertainment. A year after Pulitzer introduced the cartoon, circulation had risen 400 percent.

Then came a critical development: the shift from a subscriber base of financial support to an advertiser base of support. Perhaps more than anything, this organizational innovation turned the development of daily newspapers, in North America at least, away from the culture- and democracy-promoting interests of the early days, and toward solidly commercial interests. By underwriting the cost of scaling up print production, it also consolidated the mass-circulation newspaper as the norm.

As Innis discovered in his research, over a 50-year period from 1880 to 1930, newspapers' dependence on advertising increased from well under 50 percent (44 percent) to well over 50 percent (74 percent). Who were these advertisers? Manufacturers promoting the latest in mass-produced manufacturing products; everything from clothing and soaps which people had formerly made for themselves, to new "consumer" goods such as electric fridges, stoves and toasters. The age of mass-production and mass distribution needed the services of mass-circulation advertising and promotion to complete the mass-production circle, in the form of mass consumption. The new media of print communication was the perfect vehicle to achieve this.

By subsidizing the cost of producing a colourful exciting daily newspaper through their ads, manufacturers brought down the unit cost of the newspaper. This put it within the reach of practically everyone, certainly the middle classes.

The opposite was equally true. The mass-circulation newspaper put this massive reading public within reach of the advertisers. As Roy Thomson, the founder of the Thomson newspaper chain once observed, editorial content "is the stuff you separate the ads with."

This connection between newspaper ads and newspaper readers is what prompted Daniel Boorstin to describe newspapers as "streetcars of the mind." In the metaphor, newspaper advertisements enticing people to improve their lives and brighten their kitchens with this or that product served to transport people's minds from the residential streets where they read the newspaper to the department stores downtown where they could quickly buy these items, once they hopped on the local streetcar. The metaphor nicely anticipates communication scholar, Dallas Smythe's, references to the mass media "delivering audiences" into the hands of advertisers.

> "Newspaper civilization had entered the concluding phase of its intensive development in the speculative activity of the twenties. Its bias culminated in an obsession with the immediate. Journalism, in the words of Henry James, became a criticism of the moment at the moment." (Innis, 1984:187)

The connection with transportation was more than metaphoric. The mass-transportation facilities of the railways were critical both for delivering masses of (Canadian) newsprint to publishers, and for distributing bundles of newspapers across the country for door-to-door delivery. Finally, the telegraph, an adjunct of the railway line, was critical for delivering mass content in the form of new news every day.

News syndicates acted as pools for stories filed across the telegraph line, and suppliers of copy to papers across the country. They supported a scale-up of content and, in doing so, they supported the scale-up of production and distribution infrastructures. At the same time, they further biased the development of newspapers away from the telling of local stories to local communities, toward the buying and selling of stories as commodities. The fact that wire-story journalists, or "stringers," were paid by the word underscored the increasingly commercial nature of newspaper communication. This will be discussed later in terms of two models of communication: the transmission model versus the ritual or social-bonding model of communication.

WHAT CHANGED WITH MASS-CIRCULATION NEWSPAPERS

The development of mass-circulation newspapers and newspaper chains profoundly influenced the growth of what is commonly referred to as a mass consumer culture and society. It's useful to understand the factors in this medium's development that contributed to it. In a sense, we could call them the key messages of mass print communication, in the spirit of McLuhan's phrase, "the medium is the message."

1) The development of print media along the capital-intensive lines of mass mechanical printing presses consolidated a production model of communication and related knowledge in the areas where it was applied. These areas were the mass-circulation newspapers of popular culture and the textbook publishers associated with academic or official public knowledge. This production model featured an increasingly industrial division of labour, with a few creators as

voices of authority, and many support staff as researchers, copy editors, and so on. It also featured masses of anonymous passive readers.

2) The second message of the new media was the scale-up of communication it permitted, for those who could afford the price of admission. As A.J. Leibling commented well over half a century ago: "Freedom of the press belongs to the man who owns one." Or, as Randolph Hearst, the creator of one of the earliest national newspaper chains put it: "News is largely a matter of what one man wants the people to know and feel and think" (Innis, 1949:13). This scale-up in turn set in motion the various "rigidities" associated with large-scale systems, as discussed in Units 1 and 4. The rigidities of financing, stemming from dependency on big advertisers to pay the bills, biased production toward what would keep advertising support. The rigidities of unused capacity, associated with the need to fill the news "hole" with fresh copy every day, biased the system to constantly seek relatively quick and cheap sources of dramatic news in subject areas like natural disasters or murders. Finally, the scale-up toward instant mass communication over vast newspaper marketing areas set the stage for oligopolies and monopolies to develop around public knowledge and media communication. With structural monopolies, as discussed in Unit 1, once a high, minimal, indivisible unit of investment has been established as the requirement to enter production and compete, this standard can effectively reduce competition to only one or two big operators. Not only can few afford to operate on such a large scale, but available market demand limits participation to a few.

Frank Eager, master printer, operating a printing press at the National Museum of Science and Technology, Ottawa

3) A third message of mass print media is the inequalities built into the structures, then imposed through the structures of culture. The most dramatic of these inequalities is between the producers of knowledge and the consumers of knowledge. This has produced the taken-for-granted disparity between the authoritative "expert" and the "ignorant masses." The experts are concentrated at the centre of publishing and newspaper production, far removed from the readers of newspapers or of textbooks. They have specialized skills, sometimes speak a specialized language and have access to the structures of communication. Academics have access to academic journals and textbook publishers by virtue of being academics. Journalists have access to newspapers through employment or freelance contracts. The scaled-up messages they produce are distributed to hundreds of thousands of people, who in turn have little or no opportunity to reciprocate.

With mass-circulation newspapers (and even more so with today's multi-media conglomerates), fewer and more powerful voices of authority have come to replace a multiplicity of local voices and local and regional knowledge.

4) A fourth message of industrialized print communication is the standardization and homogenization of communication and knowledge. Partly this is achieved through a standardized alphabet translating the expressive complexity of human speech and body language into a set of uniform abstractions. Partly too, it's been achieved through the technical means of communicating quickly across vast distances using, for instance, the telegraph. The telegraph epitomizes the bias of space in its tendency to pare down human communication to the minimum required to communicate the bare facts. As James Carey spells out, fast media of communication, which the telegraph epitomizes, strip language of its expressive capacity (see Carey reading).

> "Printing from movable types created a quite unexpected new environment — it created the PUBLIC. Manuscript technology did not have the intensity or power of extension necessary to create publics on a national scale. What we have called 'nations' [nation states] in recent centuries did not, and could not, precede the advent of Gutenberg technology." (McLuhan, 1962:8)

What was a loss for particular local cultures was a gain for the newspaper industry. The simplified language was useful to newspapers wanting to reach masses of readers across the length and breadth of the continent. They needed a flattened out, standardized language that would convey basically the same message to all readers no matter what their particular cultural background. This, in turn, moulded or massaged local cultural groups into an increasingly homogenous national culture. National public opinion was the cultural product of mass-circulation newspapers and news magazines.

5) A fifth message of the new print media was the differentiation of language between public and private knowledge. The use of scientific language, objectifying experience into facts and data, came to be associated with the production of official public knowledge (what Ursula Franklin calls "constructed reality"). In turn, this consolidated the inequalities associated with the expert producers of knowledge, trained to speak and write in this objectifying manner, and non-expert readers. Not only was the message of vernacular reality, or lived experience, subtly discredited, but the authority of the experts and the expert ways of knowing was tacitly reinforced.

6) This touches on a sixth message of mass-produced, mass-distributed print communication: the dependency of people on the receiving end. If world news constitutes what it means to be informed, and if the opinions of economists and other experts are the source of that informing, people can no longer rely on

"For example, the textbooks of the United States and England pay little attention to the problems of conservation and of government ownership which are of foremost importance to a new country such as Canada. Canadians are obliged to teach the economic theory of old countries and to attempt to fit their analysis of new economic facts into an old background. The handicaps of this process are obvious, and there is evidence to show that the application of the economic theories of old countries to the problems of new countries results in a new form of exploitation with dangerous consequences." (Innis, 1956:3)

themselves and their neighbours. They depend on the national newspaper, on *Time* magazine and *Maclean's*.

Harold Innis was acutely conscious of this problem as it affected teaching Canadian economics to Canadian university students (see box).

All this shapes us as a culture, making us aware or unaware of ourselves in all our particular differences.

COMMUNICATION AND CULTURE The dictionary defines culture as "the totality of socially transmitted behaviour patterns, arts, beliefs, institutions and all other products of human work and thought characteristic of a community or population." From a social-context perspective, it can also be understood as a medium in the broadest meaning of the term (like a biological medium for culturing microorganisms). It's the communications environment that people share and through which they forge a collective existence. For Harold Innis, the critical question was that of agency, and whether people could think for themselves within this communications environment, and act on their conclusions. "Culture is concerned with the capacity of the individual to appraise problems in terms of space and time and with enabling him to take the proper steps at the right time." (Innis, 1984:85)

In a "culture of compliance," in a communications environment dominated by what Noam Chomsky and Edward Herman have called "the manufacturing of consent," this agency is seriously compromised.

WAYS OF THINKING ABOUT COMMUNICATION In traditional approaches to communication studies, these themes are sometimes obscured by the tendency to treat structures (media carriers) as separate from content. A lot of attention is paid to media ownership, with questions raised about whether a particular media owner, such as Conrad Black, is biasing editorial content, either by a heavy-handed interference in editorial hirings and firings or through direct influence on editorial content (see box). But this ignores the biases built into the commercial structures of these industries, which can be much more heavy handed than individual personalities. Furthermore, because they're built in, they're as invisible as the racist biases built into Robert Moses' New York parkway overpasses.

> In 1996 Conrad Black's media holding company, Hollinger Corp., bought a block of shares in the Southam Newspaper chain from Power Corp., gaining effective control of the company with 41 percent of the stock. Earlier in the year, Hollinger had bought 12 dailies in Atlantic Canada and Ontario from the Thomson newspaper chain.
>
> The purchases gave Hollinger Corp. control of 58 daily newspapers in Canada. Hollinger International, the American subsidiary, controls 115 daily newspapers in the US. As well, Black owns important newspapers in Britain, Australia and elsewhere, including the *Jerusalem Post.* (Saunders, Mahood and Waldie, 1996:B1)

The more materialist social-context approach to media technology allows one to see how the content is deeply influenced by the structures of media transmission.

1) In context, we see communication as a social and historical process involving values-based choices which then become hidden under the seemingly value-neutral skin of machinery. We see the ***choice paths*** involved in the growing dependence on the written and printed word, including in university education. We see the trade-offs involved in the scale-up of print communication into mass-distribution newspapers and, to a certain extent, textbooks. The flexibility and diversity associated with a plurality of small publishers and a mix of oral and print media has been traded off to a large extent in favour of a more homogenized mainstream associated with national public opinion, which the national newspaper chains and mainstream texts helped to cultivate.

2) In emphasizing the social relations involved in the interplay of media and message and how the message is received, the social-context approach allows us to see that participation in the communication process is far from equal in a media milieu dominated by mass-circulation media conglomerates. In fact, inequalities are sharpened, with a few large institutional centres of knowledge, information and opinion, and a vast hinterland or receiving area where consumers of this information don't talk back, except through letters to the editor, and now, email.

3) In context too, we see that there's a strong commercial bias in the information transmitted and received by these large media corporations. An economic model of communication predominates. Yet communication also involves social bonding. It's not just individuals exchanging information anonymously. It's people in social relationships, in communities.

If communication doesn't have an immediate commercial value, yet is valuable as public knowledge and culture, it has to be subsidized or regulated in the public interest. Hence the importance of public/state support of culture, and the communication required to sustain those social bonds. We'll return to these models in the next two units, and again in Unit 10.

COMMENTARY ON SUPPLEMENTARY READINGS

James Carey, "Technology and Ideology: The Case of the Telegraph."

There are many important insights in this reading including, in section III, the following points:

* Carey attaches great importance to the telegraph as a medium of coordination and control. The telegraph was vital in the integration of local and regional markets and the creation of national markets in support of mass-production, mass-distribution industrialization (see Unit 4).

* The telegraph fundamentally changed structures of language and public perception.

* Related to this, it represented a watershed in communication because it marked the first separation of communication from transportation. It was the first de-materialization of communication into an electric form travelling at the speed of light, not the speed of horses, or trains or other physical conveyance.

* It helped solidify the space bias in modern communication, the transmission model displacing the older religious and social-bonding views of communication. As such it helped solidify the commercial model of modern society.

* Its speed and volume and the distances between sender and receiver helped promote a depersonalization of communication, similar to the depersonalization of labour relations discussed in Unit 5.

* The anonymous relations of communication turned the telegraph into a medium for the anonymous control and coordination of business.

* The mythic ideology pervading the telegraph ("the electric sublime") mitigated this anonymity, by exalting the technology as progressive.

* Focusing on the transformative effects on language and particularly in newspapers (III), Carey notes that speeding up communication and stretching language over long-distance telegraph lines demanded and imposed changes in the language. One of these was standardization; another was abbreviation. An involved fiduciary relationship of communication (an extension of the conversation format into letters of correspondence) was replaced by a remote conveyance of dispassionate facts.

* This depersonalization of communication was accompanied by an industrial or production-model approach to it, with news becoming raw material (supplied by stringers, not correspondents) via telegraph, which was assembled and packaged into stories in a factory-like newsroom.

* The telegraph emphasized the separation of the mind from the body, including the body of physical geography, and began the process now known as virtual reality. It fostered the emergence of wholly mental spaces, separated from organic and physical places. The first example of these was the futures market.

* This also had the effect of consolidating a new realm of perception populated by commodities and prices, as though these were real in their own right, and no longer attached to living people and places.

QUESTIONS FOR DISCUSSION

Go back to the questions posed at the beginning of the unit and see how well you can answer them now. Then, consider some of the following additional questions:

1) Is communicating by email similar to communicating by telegraph? What similarities do you sense, what differences, and what accounts for these?
2) How many of the factors involved in the development of mass-circulation newspapers were also involved in the development of radio and television? Are other choice paths in these media still available?

SOURCES AND FURTHER READINGS

Carey, James, 1975. "Canadian Communication Theory: Extensions and Interpretations of Harold Innis," in *Studies in Canadian Communications*. G.J. Robinson and D. Theall, eds. Montreal: McGill Studies in Communications.

Carey, James, 1989. *Communication as Culture*. Boston: Unwin Hyman.

Fiske, John, 1990. *Introduction to Communication Studies*. London: Routledge.

Herman, Edward and Chomsky, Noam, 1988. *Manufacturing Consent: The Political Economy of the Mass Media*. New York: Pantheon Books.

Innis, Harold, 1949. *The Press: A Neglected Factor in the Economic History of the Twentieth Century*. London: Oxford University Press.

Innis, Harold, 1956. *Essays in Canadian Economic History*. Toronto: University of Toronto Press.

Martin, Carol, 1994. "Book Sale," *Canadian Forum*, 74(834).

McLuhan, Marshall, 1962. *The Gutenberg Galaxy*. Toronto: University of Toronto Press.

Saunders, John, Mahood, Casey and Waldie, Paul, 1996. "Black Reigns," The *Globe and Mail* (June 1), B1.

Taras, David, 1990. *The Newsmakers: The Media's Influence on Canadian Politics*. Toronto: Nelson.

CHAPTER 8

THE MEDIUM IS THE MESSAGE, AND THE MASSAGE

OVERVIEW

This unit takes a brief look at three other media that figure in the emerging global village of merged multi-media communication. These are radio, television (plus cable) and film. As with Unit 7, the goal here is to apply some of the ways of thinking about technology in a material sense to the mass media of contemporary culture. The idea too is to think of the social and cultural shaping power these media systems have.

Each case also emphasizes particular themes explored throughout this course. In the history of radio, for instance, we will examine the contingencies or choice paths cultivated in the early days, and what institutional agents influenced the emergence of one as predominant. In the film industry, we'll look at the growth of large-scale integrated systems of production, distribution and delivery, and the results of these in terms of dependency and the underdevelopment of Canadian film making. In television, we'll look at the emergence of community-access cable and how this was blocked from becoming a fully realized alternative model for culture and communication.

Throughout these examples, we'll look at the two models of communication discussed briefly in the previous unit: the commercial transmission model and the social-bonding model of community building. The history of media in the modern era is, in fact, a history of the struggle between these two models. At times too, the state has negotiated a compromise between them, resulting in what has become known as the mixed-model (private sector, public sector) of Canadian media and culture. In exploring these models, we'll continue to explore the bias of space at work in these media. Equally, we'll see how the more spiritual values of the time bias also continue to operate, for example, in the more holistic practice of Canadian film making.

We'll also look at the role of the state supporting certain models of media practice over others. Finally, we'll look at the media in terms of cultural environments. We'll contrast the more traditional grounded environments of face-to-face communication and local community with the emerging environments of space. The media landscapes, or mediascapes, created by the new electronic media can be seen to create a parallel universe in which you and I constitute ourselves as "subjects" through vicarious involvement in television dramas. For some, this mediaspace is more real and compelling than the dramas gripping their own local community. This has consequences that deserve our critical attention.

OBJECTIVES

At the end of this unit, you should be able to answer the following questions:

1) What choice paths were there in the development of radio in Canada, and what influenced the emergence of a dominant path?
2) How does vertical integration operate in the North American film industry?
3) What are the differences between the commodity-transmission model and the social-bonding model of communication?

THE ORIGINAL TERM used to describe radio, radiotelephony, is revealing. The earliest radios were a wireless extension of the telephone, and the telephone was a tool of one-to-one communication. So it's not surprising that the first uses of radio were for personal communication too. The earliest amateur radio operators, who bought or assembled both transmitting and receiving equipment, created their own sub-culture rather like the Internet enthusiasts of the 1970s and early '80s. There was no distinction (nor related inequalities) between producers and consumers. For those who could afford the equipment and acquire the skills to participate, everyone participated equally. Slowly, though, the broadcasting possibilities attracted the interest of groups with a message to spread. One of the most dramatic early examples of this was in the 1916 Irish Uprising, when Irish nationalists used a ship's wireless to broadcast news of their cause, hoping to gain sympathy, especially among ex-patriate Irish in the United States. However, the spreading of commercial messages and images would soon become the norm.

CONTINGENCY AND THE DEVELOPMENT OF RADIO The early years of the 20th century, particularly the 1920s, saw a tremendous flowering of cultural institutions, especially ones with a pan-Canadian focus. The Canadian Teachers' Federation, the Canadian Federation of University Women's Clubs, the Student Christian Movement (the first national organization of university students), the Canadian Authors' Association and the Canadian Chambers of Commerce. In one year alone, 1927, the number of Canadian clubs more than doubled, from 53 to 120 (Prang, 1965:2).

In this climate of activist, participative cultural practice, many groups saw the radio as a means of reaching a wider population base, especially in rural Canada. Some groups formed radio societies. Some universities and some churches started their own radio stations, getting licenses for transmitters from the federal Department of Marine.

At the same time, though, businesses associated with the burgeoning electricity and electric-appliance industries were busily selling receivers, and trying to enlarge this market. An employee of the Canadian Marconi Company, Max Smith, gave this contingency path a boost with his idea of developing entertaining content with which to lure would-be buyers of radio receivers. Canadian Marconi put Max Smith on the air with the first commercial radio station in Canada, XWA (later CFCF) of Montreal, in 1920 (Peers, 1967:5). That same year, Westinghouse inaugurated the first commercial radio station in the US by broadcasting the results of the Harding-

Cox presidential election. The shift from holistic participatory communication to the production and transmission of product had begun.

In the development, or enterprise, stage of radio, the two contingency paths continued to expand, although the commercial path took a clear and early lead. By 1923, licenses had been issued to 62 private commercial stations and to eight amateur stations, although the private stations ended up dwindling to something like 34 that actually went on air. According to Frank Peers' detailed history of Canadian broadcasting, nearly every commercial station was operated either by a company selling radio equipment, such as Marconi and Westinghouse, or by a newspaper. These included the *Toronto Star* (with CFCA), the *Vancouver Province*, the two Winnipeg papers, the *Free Press* and the *Tribune*, and *La Presse* in Montreal (Peers, 1967:6).

CBC microphone.
National Museum of Science and Technology

This development introduced an interesting element of scale and rigidity. Both sets of corporations had already established themselves on the large scale associated with commercial industrialization. The rigidities of their financing propelled them to keep expanding their market base, by selling new products and reaching out to new audiences. In turn, they could spread the costs of the new radio operation across their entire operating system, and sometimes also recycle material from one medium to another.

But there was another factor that influenced commercial radio development in Canada: the branch-plant or "affiliated station." Many Canadian stations never developed much Canadian content and programming, but simply hooked themselves into the American radio networks, as "affiliates."

While Canadians operated a few dozen stations by the mid-1920s, there were over 550 stations in the United States. Furthermore, many were organized into large-scale systems similar to newspaper chains: radio networks. One was the NBC Broadcasting, a subsidiary of the Radio Corporation of America (RCA), a partnership between General Electric and Westinghouse. The other was the Columbia Broadcasting System (CBS) (Peers, 1967:10).

Margaret Prang's history of Canadian broadcasting notes that half the Canadian broadcasting power was concentrated in Montreal and Toronto, where "several of the stations devoted a high proportion of their time to relaying American programmes sponsored by American commercial interests doing business in Canada" (Prang, 1965:4). The branch-plant pattern in Canadian industrial development, where the biggest names in manufactured products were American, was mirrored in the development of commercial radio.

From the earliest days, too, the airspace created by radio waves was continental in scale. For example, in the 1920s, the Canadian government agreed to share 11 radio channels with American programmers, keeping only six clear channels for Canadian stations. And even there, Canadian stations were often drowned out because the average signal strength was considerably weaker than that of the American stations. The *Toronto Star*'s CFCA, which had the only clear signal in Toronto and at least broadcast a semblance of a daily program, operated with a 100-watt transmitter. By contrast, in 1928, 40 American stations were licensed with a power of between 5,000 and 25,000 watts. Toronto's CKGW, one of two Canadian stations with 5,000-watt transmitters, had to share its channel space with American stations and consequently could broadcast for only part of each day (Peers, 1967:21).

As a result, the majority of Canadians with licenses for receiving equipment, most of whom were in or near urban centres, were listening to American rather than Canadian programs. These included the more popular programs such as the comedy show "Amos 'n Andy," compared to which Canadian programming was seen as "inferior." By the end of the 1920s, at least 80 percent of the programs to which Canadians listened were of American origin (Prang, 1965:4).

Still, there was a national Canadian network. The radio department of Canadian National Railways, which was then a public railway company formed when the government took over several faltering or failed private railway companies, including the Grand Trunk and the Intercolonial, inaugurated the first national Canadian radio broadcast in 1927, with a speech by Prime Minister William Lyon MacKenzie King celebrating the Diamond Jubilee of Confederation. The event was one of several suggestions for celebrating the Jubilee put forward by the executive of the Association of Canadian Clubs, the secretary of which was Graham Spry, an avid Canadian culture supporter.

By 1929, CNRO was broadcasting three hours a day across the country, including comic operas, school broadcasts and concerts, and had broadcasting contracts with the Hart House Quartet at the University of Toronto and the Toronto Symphony Orchestra. Canadian Pacific Railway was also contemplating its own private network (Peers, 1967:24).

THE STATE AND PUBLIC/PRIVATE BROADCASTING The development of radio in Canada offers some important insights into the role of the state and federal/provincial powers in directing the choice paths of development, whether economic or cultural. One of the more popular views of the state is the liberal view, which sees it as a neutral instrument of the national will. A contrasting view is the dependency view in which the state is seen as a tool of international capital and its associates in the local bourgeoisie. And a third view falls somewhere in between, with the state playing something of a mediating role among various vested interests (Albo and Jensen, 1989:180-206).

The history of broadcasting in Canada tends to support the third view, while also shedding some very revealing light on the importance of bureaucracy. In 1928, Prime Minister MacKenzie King appointed a commission of inquiry into creating a Canadian broadcasting system. It was known as the Aird Commission after its chief commissioner, Sir John Aird, president of the Canadian Bank of Commerce. Its other two commissioners were Charles Bowman, editor of the *Ottawa Citizen* and Dr. August Frigon, director of technical education for Quebec. The commission looked at the British broadcasting system, where radio was clearly established as a public service with annual receiver licenses distributed by the post office, and it looked at the American system, which was vehemently commercial with broadcast licenses initially dispensed by the US Secretary of Commerce. A year later, it reported back, recommending a national broadcasting system to be operated as a public utility. Some of the key recommendations were:

1) A wholly public infrastructure for radio broadcasting. A public company would own and operate all radio stations, and would build and maintain a network of seven 50,000-watt stations across the country to provide service "to all Canadians."
2) Provincial directors of this company would have "full control" of programs broadcast within their respective provinces. Not surprisingly, this recommendation owed a lot to Dr. Frigon's presence on the inquiry.
3) The company would be funded by a combination of revenues from license fees, indirect advertising (companies sponsoring programs, but not advertising on them) and government subsidy. Initially, a $3 a year fee was proposed for radio receiver licenses. At the time, Canadians were paying about $1.

By the time the forerunner of the CBC was formed, in 1932, all three of these principles had been seriously diminished if not betrayed. It was partly the result of the Depression, which diminished confidence as well as public finances. It was partly, too, due to private-sector pressure and propaganda by commercial radio, on their airwaves, including a claim that people would have to pay $30 a year in license fees to listen to "civil service radio" (Prang,

1965:16). And it was partly due to the election of a Conservative government more responsive particularly to Toronto business leaders (such as F.R. MacKelcan, legal counsel with the National Trust) who lobbied to preserve an advertising-based model of radio. The CBC's organizational structure featured strong centralized federal control over both general policy and everyday management. Its financial arrangements reduced the annual license fee from $3 to $2, yet failed to provide for adequate and sustainable government support to fill the gap. And so, by default, the plan to have a wholly public infrastructure was abandoned, and local commercial stations proliferated.

However, a public radio network was created, largely due to the public-interest groups who'd taken an early interest in radio as a tool of culture and community building. This group, called the Canadian Radio League, was conceived by Graham Spry, national secretary of the Association of Canadian Clubs, after the defeat of the Liberals in the 1930 election threatened to bury the Aird Commission in the dust of the Great Depression. Between Spry, as chairman, and Alan Plaunt, as secretary, the league rallied the support of national voluntary organizations, women's groups, farmer organizations, unions, educational and other cultural institutions, plus leading Canadian newspapers and even businessmen not affiliated with American branch plants (see box).

> "All the invader has to pay for is his station and wires ... his program is built for an audience twenty or forty times as large as yours and therefore costs him infinitely less from the standpoint of returns.... The invading advertiser may in time pre-empt all the best hours on our biggest stations and ... even our own wave channels will be closed to us." (Advertising manager of Imperial Oil Company in letter to Plaunt, 10 Dec. 1930, quoted in Prang, 1965:18)

For Spry and the Canadian Radio League, the struggle between a commercial and a public model of radio communication came down to "the state or the United States." (Prang, 1965:28) To counter the scale of commercialism US industry could command, state intervention was essential. And as Spry's vision prevailed, so did a particular pan-Canadian vision of Canadian identity, informed more by the need to stand together against American commercialism than the particulars of locality, religion, race and ethnic origin, gender, class or other shared experience.

> "Regional and racial divisions had yielded to a national unity, long in the process of growth, but brought to fresh consciousness by a new American threat." (Prang, 1965:31)

CANADIAN FILMS AND THE HOLLYWOOD PRODUCTION MODEL Ten years ago, most students taking this course only mentioned American movies when asked to name their favourite movies, unless they were taking a Film Studies course. Now many Canadian titles come to mind: *Margaret's Museum*, *Crash*, *The Decline* *of the American Empire, Jesus of Montreal, Hard Core Logo, Highway 61, I Heard the Mermaids Singing, Exotica.* Canadian directors and producers are also better known: Patricia Rozema, Aton Egoyam, Robert Lepage, Denis Arcands, Bruce McDonald. But for a Canadian to see a Canadian movie is still a bit like sighting a rare bird. Less than 5 percent of the total screen time of the 1,700 movie screens available to Canadians across the country is devoted to Canadian films. A Toronto survey done in 1996 found that Canadian films accounted for less than 2 percent of first-run screens. Quebec screen share is higher, at about 3.36 percent of revenues (Everett-Green, 1997:C2).

Overall, the picture on the big screen is not very Canadian. This is because even when Canadian films, such as Pierre Gang's *Sous-Sol* and Bruce McDonald's *Hard Core Logo*, win prestigious film awards in Canada and around the world, they are largely excluded from the major theatre chains. That's been the problem with Canadian cinema since the beginning (Everett-Green, 1997:C2). A large-scale industrial production model was established in the 1920s, augmented by large-scale distribution and exhibition, all controlled by Hollywood, its industry association, the Motion Picture Association of America, and its international arm, the Motion Picture Export Association of America.

One of the earliest Canadian developments in the fledgling movie business was the consolidation of investment in the distribution/exhibition end rather than the creative end of production. This became significant as those early business initiatives became linked to the larger American production system, which severed any ties of common vested interest with Canadian film producers. This set the pattern for the "dependent development" of Canada's film industry (Pendakur, 1990:45). The first example of this was the Allens, who began exhibiting films in storefront screens and also distributing films in the early years of this century. In 1915, they suddenly expanded into a national distributing network based on obtaining an exclusive franchise to distribute Paramount movies out of Hollywood. This became the Famous Players chain of theatres. By the 1920s, the pattern of Canadian distributors serving as (exclusive) distribution arms of the major Hollywood studios was deeply entrenched. Furthermore, Canadian businessmen associated with these chains had invested heavily in the palatial theatres the Hollywood majors promoted to ensure large mass audiences for the first runs of their movies. And the rigidities associated with these investments, particularly that of *unused capacity*, biased theatre owners toward a ready steady supply of films with which to stock their theatres, and a commercially appealing film product that would keep drawing a large mass audience.

By the mid-1920s, the fledgling Canadian film industry was almost snuffed out, and the independent (non-branch plant) Canadian exhibitors and distributors were poised to follow suit. A federal commission into what seemed to be a Hollywood-based combine or monopoly recommended a quota of 25 percent of screen time in Canadian theatres for Canadian films. However this was foiled by the Motion Picture Exhibitors and Distributors of Canada, which Joyce Nelson has described as "a local bureau" of the American MPAA (Nelson, 1988:81). The president of this putatively Canadian distributors' organization, Col. John Cooper, was quoted (by Nelson) as saying that "the profits of the motion picture industry in Canada are in running theatres, not in making and distributing motion pictures."

A BRIEF HISTORY OF CINEPLEX ODEON

In 1979, Garth Drabinsky and N.A. Taylor launched a new Canadian theatre chain, called Cineplex. By 1982, Cineplex had access to 149 screens in 13 cities, and was suddenly cut off from access to first-run American films by all the Hollywood majors. Two years later, Cineplex, with financing from Charles Bronfman, bought up the Canadian Odeon theatre chain. Drabinsky then went into a distribution partnership with MCA, the parent of Universal Pictures under which MCA acquired a 50 percent interest in the Cineplex Odeon chain, which by 1987 had become the largest theatre chain in North America (Pendakur, 1988:16-17).

Once the monopoly scale of vertically integrated production, distribution and exhibition was established, an actual conspiracy or combine was hardly necessary. The sheer scale of the operation excluded all but those who could afford to operate on such a large commercial scale. The scale of investment also established what has become known as the Hollywood standard in film making: a glitzy product with lots of action, scenery and other sensory riches for audiences to consume. While the average American movie costs $27 million to make, the average Canadian movie has a budget of less than $5 million, and often less than half of that (Everett-Green, 1997:C1).

As with radio, the commercial bias of space triumphed over the more spiritual values of time, memory and public culture in shaping the dominant patterns in film. Film making in the Hollywood tradition closely follows an industrial production model, with rigid hierarchies, prescribed roles and a culture of compliance. The integrated chains of distribution and exhibition support this with a transmission model of communication, geared to getting the greatest amount of "product" to the largest possible consumer-audience base as fast as possible. Meanwhile, its advertising arm, augmented with cross-genre and cereal-box promotions, hypes the latest release to keep audiences coming back.

But culture as consumption hadn't triumphed totally. Increasingly, Canadian film makers had been turning their backs on the Hollywood production model. From the earliest days of Canadian film making, and especially in the period from the 1970s to the 1990s, Canadian film makers, and their audiences, have cultivated a more participative model of culture and communication. As the video interview with media-arts curator and critic, Sue Ditta, demonstrated, they have done this through a lot of self-help organizational structures and with some important support from the state. Some of the points to emerge from that interview are worth repeating here:

* The communication model is fundamentally different in this Canadian tradition of film making. Instead of anonymous mass-market audiences, the viewers of these films are seen as members of a particular community with which the film maker is in communication. It's not quite conversational, but something of this dialogue is suggested.

* In keeping with this notion of addressing particular audiences rather than homogenized mass audiences, the films are radically diverse and distinct in their differences. They speak to the particularities of geographic place as well as race and ethnicity, sexuality, class and life experience.

* Film festivals are a major site for the exhibition of Canadian films. These festivals are geared to more of a participatory role for audience members, rather than the passive role associated with going to the theatre chains.

* Film and video co-ops have been an important innovation, allowing film makers to work together and to make films in a supportive atmosphere.

* Funding support from the state — through Telefilm Canada, for example — has been critical.

* There is a continuing crisis associated with a lack of "public" screens where Canadian films can beat the shut-out by Canadian theatre chains, and cultivate a sustainable financial base through a regular audience. Winning awards at festivals doesn't pay the bills.

MONOPOLY-SCALE MEDIASCAPES AND IDENTITY The pattern that developed in mainstream television was similar to the pattern just discussed for film. The dominant pattern has featured a few large-scale production and distribution networks, with Canadian television and cable interests concentrating on distribution, and on keeping those distribution lines filled to capacity. Their dependency on a steady supply of product with which to attract a mass scale of audience, in order to sell advertising slots at the highest possible rate, has in turn reinforced their dependency on American product. Furthermore, this product has been priced at attractively low rates, considering the glitzy production values and the high production costs, because the monopoly scale of the networks' operations allows them to spread the cost over both the US market and its burgeoning international market. Almost from the beginning, this market has included Canadian networks licensed to broadcast big-name American shows (Nelson, 1986-7:12). That's why Canadian content is such a joke on Canadian commercial television, peaking at less than 40 percent during prime time, although national and local news programs are included in the count.

What does this mean for culture and identity? There's a lot of talk of the Americanization of Canadian culture, and from the evidence of the mainstream mass media, this is clearly true. On the other hand, there's the countervailing evidence of community-access television, community radio, native broadcasting, Canadian film festivals, and so on, which occupy a large, if unintegrated space apart from this mainstream. More importantly is the homogenization and passivity associated with the "couch potato" image of the TV addict. McLuhan was one of the first cultural critics to speak of the social-conditioning effects of television. This new "extension of man" created a wrap-around acoustic space or sensory environment that drew people into it. It eroded individuality and replaced it with a new tribalism, the beginnings of a collective consciousness he predicted would mature in the computer age.

Television sets for sale.
Future Shop, Ottawa

The medium is the message, and the massage, he said. It creates a spatial environment that mediates people's sense of themselves through the biases built into that environment.

It's important, however, to test all the assumptions associated with focusing on these corporate media systems. It's important to turn the frame around, or at least to broaden it to include culture and communication outside these large-scale media systems. It's important, for example, to remember the oral culture of everyday life where people first share their experiences, first learn to tell and listen to stories: a first circle of family and friends, the first teenage hang-outs, the cafés and bars that sometimes become the particular gathering place for people sharing various points of difference. Many media developments that fit the non-commercial, community-building model of communication are extensions of this dynamic, organic participatory oral culture.

Native radio and television are prime illustrations of this. Examples include:

1) the Aboriginal Multi-Media Society of Alberta, which broadcasts weekly programs in Cree to some 46 native communities in Northern Alberta out of its studios in Lac La Biche, and also publishes a biweekly newspaper out of Edmonton;

2) the Innuit Broadcasting Corporation. Using the Anik 2 satellite system, this native broadcaster, established in 1982, produces over three hours of programming a week, in Inuktitut, and broadcasts it to some 30,000 people in over 25 communities across the Arctic. With the withdrawal of funding from Telefilm Canada in 1995, the IBC has been severely cut back, but was endeavouring to translate its popular children's programs into English for sale in southern markets.

3) small FM stations in native communities, such as CKHQ at Kanehsatake and CKRK in Kahnawake. As communication scholar, Lorna Roth, has written, these radio stations played a crucial role in communication during the 1990 Oka crisis, both within native communities and across cultural boundaries. When the Canadian Armed forces had surrounded the native community of Kanehsatake at Oka and slowly imposed a news blackout on the native protesters, two native broadcasters, Marie David and Bev Nelson, camped out at the station so they could continue broadcasting news from inside, via their tiny 10-watt transmitter. They supplemented this through phone and fax connections to national and international support groups, with feeds from their broadcasts sometimes supplied to other stations. Meanwhile, the CKRK radio station at Kahnawake, located on a reserve on the south shore of Montreal, found that with its more powerful 50-watt transmitter, it had both an insider audience of native residents on the reserve and a growing number of outsiders living in Montreal and southern Quebec. Its news supplied an alternative source of information on the stand-off with the natives protesting the conversion of sacred native land into a golf course at Oka. Its phone-in show, called *The Party Line,* promoted "cross-cultural communication" and solidarity (Roth, 1993:320).

These two small radio stations represented a fascinating example of what Lorna Roth describes as "mediaspace as a site for struggle over dominant meanings ..."(Roth, 1993:317)

The question is, do they make a difference? And how could they? This will be discussed further in Unit 9, in terms of monopolies of knowledge and in Unit 10, in terms of design alternatives for the information society.

COMMENTARY ON SUPPLEMENTARY READINGS

Dot Tuer, "All in the Family: An Examination of Community Access Cable in Canada."

This is an excellent essay for both the details of how community access cable was designed to fail, as well as the social-shaping power (the massaging power) of mass-media television. Note some of the following points in particular:

* As she's writing this piece on community access cable and its importance, she's constantly reminded that nothing from this form of television has stayed in her own consciousness. Instead, she is swamped by memories of the mainstream television she watched every day and every week as she grew up. She's surprised at the social-bonding power these stories have had. She's surprised at her own personal entanglement in the mediaspace that is both "very local and vastly global" because it was such a fixture of family life where and when she grew up.

* Cable television was introduced with the twin idea of being a medium of local programming as well as a monopoly for broadcasting regular TV within a particular district.

* Except in Quebec where community groups were themselves given a license to broadcast over the local cable-access station, thus exercising direct control over programming themselves, the licenses went to commercial companies interested in the cable distribution of mainstream television programs. They added local production facilities to meet the "community" requirements for getting their license.

* Though the National Film Board spent its earliest years as a quasi-propaganda tool for Canada and the British Empire and Commonwealth, a metamorphosis was evident in the post-World War II era. It became Canadian in its focus, and actively promoted self-knowledge and identity within Canada's particular communities. The people associated with its grassroots *Challenge for Change* series saw cable as the perfect medium for community culture and grassroots communication. So they supported the efforts of a Thunder Bay community to open up municipal politics through its "Town Hall" program. The program's success was marked by moves to clip its wings. And the power of the cable license holder over community groups doing programming became clear in a set of rules requiring all material to be pre-packaged and submitted for approval as properly "balanced." Censorship, in the name of "balance" or "community standards" has continued to be an issue.

* Efforts by community groups to get a license from the CRTC for their own broadcast facilities have failed. As Tuer points out, this drove home the point that community cable (a participatory, com-

munity-building model of communication) was not to be developed as a *parallel* structure to the commercial model, but as a niche *contained by* and within the commercial structures. As Kim Goldberg put it, community programming is "a democratic concept without a democratic structure."

* Without separate funding, programming was left to volunteer labour, with the predictable results in the form of burn-out and uneven quality.

* The CRTC's ruling in 1971 that local programming meant that programs couldn't be shared in a network of community cable television (the no "bicycling" rule) aggravated this. Not only were local programmers blocked from a source of cost-recovery revenue. They were blocked from developing a parallel distribution network that could reach a critical mass of audiences, and actually challenge the mainstream. Finally, the mandate that community programming address particularized interest groups within the community rather than a general audience blocked community cable programmers from challenging the images associated with the general audience and the cultural mainstream even locally. Ultimately, each particular group was kept in its own particular niche of difference.

* These issues of infrastructure, and who plans how these will function, intimately influence how the media is contextualized as a medium communicating identity. It was contextualized as a medium of the nuclear family, not of the community, Tuer says. Now, in the move to the 500-channel universe, it's possibly being recontextualized as a medium of the atomized, individualized consumer.

QUESTIONS FOR DISCUSSION

1) How is broadcasting in Canada an example of a mixed-model approach in cultural policymaking?
2) From the evidence of Canadian media and film policy, has the state stood up for the Canadian people at large, or more for certain interest groups within the country?
3) What has vertical integration in the film industry in Canada meant for Canadian film makers and audiences?

SOURCES AND FURTHER READINGS

Albo, Gregory and Jenson, Jane, 1989. "The Relative Autonomy of the State," in *The New Canadian Political Economy*. Wallace Clement and Glen Williams, eds. Montreal: McGill-Queen's University Press.

Everett-Green, Robert, 1997. "Not Coming Soon to a Theatre Near You," The *Globe and Mail* (January 18).

Nelson, Joyce, 1986/87. "CRTC Asleep at the Wheel," *Fuse* Magazine (Winter).

Nelson, Joyce, 1988. *The Colonized Eye: Rethinking the Grierson Legend*. Toronto: Between the Lines.

Peers, Frank, 1969. *The Politics of Canadian Broadcasting, 1920-1951*. Toronto: University of Toronto Press.

Pendakur, Manjunath, 1990. *Canadian Dreams and American Control*. Detroit: Wayne State University Press.

Pendakur, Manjunath, 1988. "Free Trade Anxieties and National Institutions," *Cinema Canada* (March).

Prang, Margaret, 1965. "The Origins of Public Broadcasting in Canada," *Canadian Historical Review* 46(1).

Roth, Lorna, 1993. "Mohawk Airwaves and Cultural Challenges: Some Reflections on the Politics of Recognition and Cultural Appropriation after the Summer of 1990," *Canadian Journal of Communication*, vol. 18.

Tuer, Dot, 1994. "All in The Family: An Examination of Community Access Cable in Canada," *Fuse* Magazine (Spring).

CHAPTER 9

MAKING AND BREAKING MONOPOLIES OF KNOWLEDGE

OVERVIEW

The point of this chapter is to give you a sense of what happens when one pattern of media structure and practice becomes dominant to the point of rigidity and monopoly. Instead of always opening up knowledge and perception through new information, knowledge itself can become rigid, with dangerous consequences.

This is possibly the most challenging unit in the course, because it's the most purely conceptual. However, it is also simply one more extension of the basic ideas discussed earlier, including large-scale systems called structural monopolies. This unit looks at how knowledge monopolies can develop around print media, then extends this to see how they might also develop around the new media of database and Internet publishing.

The unit begins with the basics in creating monopolies and oligopolies around knowledge and public perception. It then spells out the three dimensions along which these monopolies operate: the physical dimension of speed, the structural dimension of organization and the cultural dimension of how things are framed as relevant or irrelevant in the first place. Then it invites you to examine how these dimensions can be seen to operate in some of our more familiar media, such as news and the movies. It also explores how these can operate within the context of formal university education.

The unit ends by considering the possibility of breaking monopolies of knowledge, perception and communication, and what this means for a stable democratic society. As examples, it looks at the plethora of magazines speaking to particular communities of interest outside the mainstream. It also looks at the evidence of Canadian film making and the traditions discussed in Unit 8 which would suggest a breakthrough from the monopoly structures and the monopoly preconceptions of what good film making is all about. It looks too at monopolies of knowledge in public-policy discussions or discourse, taking the Berger Inquiry into the MacKenzie Valley pipeline as an example. Finally, anticipating the discussion of global communication networks creating a global-village media space at the end of the 20th century, it looks at an attempt to break the monopoly of Western news media by various smaller "third-world" countries.

OBJECTIVES

At the end of this unit, you should be able to address, if not answer, the following questions:

1) How does a physical monopoly of knowledge operate through today's news media?
2) How can structural monopolies of knowledge develop in university curricula or through university libraries?
3) How did Justice Thomas Berger break monopolies of knowledge associated with public planning and policymaking?

In the interest of making myself understood, the text in this chapter will follow the video more closely than in most other units. I will begin with the idea of someone "monopolizing" a conversation. Most of us have had some experience with this. Someone hogs the airspace, as we say. He or she cuts others off, constantly takes the conversation back to the topic this person wants to discuss, and by sheer personality, or bullying, gets everyone to go along with this.

The example illustrates nearly all the aspects of monopolies of knowledge and communication we will discuss here. The full-speed-ahead talking style that cuts others off touches on the physical aspect, the channelling of discussion fits the structural, and the outcome touches on the cultural aspect, including the consent to tolerate this.

In the holistic context of conversation, there is something we can do to prevent this hogging or monopolizing from happening because oral communication is organic, not mechanical, and therefore more subject to remote control. Also, being alive to the process of communication, it is inherently more open to change. The situation shifts dramatically with the more formal, organized and mechanized media of print, television and film, particularly as these take the form of large-scale systems of communication with distance and differences of social power separating the receiver from the sender. It also changes as communication takes the form of produced, packaged information. The hogging of what is communicated happens through speed, with faster forms of communication literally cutting off other voices telling other stories through slower forms of communication. It also happens through the scale and scope of communication, where certain sources of information are more accessible than others and thereby channel what is learned, or communicated. And it happens through the values and assumptions at work in the choice of what information should be packaged as relevant knowledge, and people's willingness to abide by these choices.

Monopolies of communication have many features. Some are familiar from previous discussions of structural monopolies, the Hudson's Bay Company and the CPR being two of the more familiar Canadian examples. Here, the critical thing is the scale of financial investment and the rigidities associated with ensuring a return on that investment by keeping the communication lines full, and how monopolies help to ensure this by restricting competition to those who can afford a high minimal fixed cost of getting established.

Many of the structural characteristics that feature in monopolies of knowledge are also familiar from previous discussions of monopoly-scale industrial structures; features such as scale, centralized control and a hierarchial division of labour. Speed as a feature has been implied more than it's been stressed, but now it emerges as an important cultural dynamic. Some of the cultural aspects, notably the commercial bias toward commodity consumption, have also been suggested in earlier units, particularly the preceding two dealing with media as a medium of identity. But here they'll be explored in more detail.

Overall, monopolies of knowledge and perception drive home Marshall McLuhan's points about the medium being the message and about media serving simultaneously as extensions of the human mind and as auto-amputations. As the knowledge (and related values) of certain minds are extended through textbooks, newspapers, television and multi-media, other minds (and related values) can be effectively amputated, or at least muted to the point of mere private opinion and chatter.

> "For the message of any medium or technology is the change of scale, pace or pattern that it introduces into human affairs." (McLuhan, 1964:24)

BASICS OF MONOPOLIES OF KNOWLEDGE Monopolies in this sense aren't huge conspiracy theories. They're much more mundane, and subtle, than that. Let's start by reiterating what's required for a monopoly to exist. A monopoly can only be created where people are dependent on an external supply. In our case, they depend on outside experts for information, on Hollywood movies for entertainment, or on textbooks for accredited knowledge. In other words, the monopoly occurs where people cannot inform themselves, entertain themselves or educate themselves on their own. Of course, this dependency can be cultivated. This is where the "cultural" aspects of monopolies of knowledge and perception come in.

Structures associated with getting and communicating knowledge buttress this dependency, as the stethoscope in an examining room illustrates quite nicely. With me, at least, the doctor always seems to cut me off mid-sentence as I'm explaining about the pain in my chest or whatever, and applies the stethoscope to my chest. In that action, I am cut off as a person and become a patient dependent on the doctor. The doctor is licensed to use the stethoscope and to interpret the information it gives him or her as the expert, and it is this knowledge that establishes what's wrong with me.

There are three dimensions of monopolies of knowledge:

1) Physical Monopolies of Knowledge:

This dimension has to do with the pace of communication rather than the scale of its structures. A monopoly of knowledge can be created physically if communication can be speeded up. The information conveyed through a faster medium of communication gets to the public first, and creates critical first impressions. The monopoly is confirmed if this fast-arriving information then becomes the basis for decision making, and the later-arriving information is relegated to the garbage as worthless "old news."

The telegraph was the key to creating monopolies of knowledge for newspaper chains in the late 19th century, through their use of telegraphed "wire copy." Not only could the telegraph communicate news quickly, but its relatively cheap and easy physical nature (compare tapping out the pulses of morse code to chiselling words onto stone) also made it easy to send a continuous supply of information as news. And so "Extra, Extra, read all about it" became the rallying cry of competing newspapers proffering the latest news.

Today, the satellite has replaced the telegraph. Media companies like CNN, which can muster a global system of satellite communication, can use that instant globe-spanning speed to monopolize the screens of public perception with the images and sound bites it collects from hot news spots around the world. Historically, CNN's satellite-based system of instant global news came into its own during the 1990 Persian Gulf War. What was within the range of its television cameras and microphones was beamed to the major media networks around the world, and those images defined "what's happening" in that war. It was months later that freelance journalists and film makers on the ground got their more in-depth stories of what happened out to the world. A video documentary, *Ecowars*, prepared by a Canadian environmental group revealed the devastation of the land and natural life through the bombing and oil-well fires. But by the time these images were released, the pace and speed of communication associated with the dominant news media had propelled the agenda of news on to other sites and other stories. That news story was dead and the war was over, though the fires blazed on. The fast-moving eyes and ears of these global news and communication systems had moved on, taking their monopoly on informing mass news audiences with them.

2) Structural Monopolies of Knowledge:

This dimension of monopolies of knowledge should be the most familiar from previous discussions of structural monopolies and monopoly-scale production systems. As with any technology, communication systems can be designed to be open and pluralistic, or they can be designed to foster centralized control and prescriptive channelling of perception. The latter is a recipe for oligopolies or monopolies of knowledge, where perception, knowledge and communication are structurally controlled by a few (oligopoly) or by a single source.

You can also spot the potential for monopoly in the structuring of university curricula and, within programs, the channelling of learning around core courses and, sometimes, one or two core texts. In monopolies of this kind, it isn't that other knowledge is shut out altogether; it's just marginalized, so that the core or mainstream of knowledge and learning fosters certain dominant impressions. One example is the concept that exporting staples is a stepping-stone to development in young countries, not a recipe for underdevelopment and dependency; or that history is primarily made by men, not women, and by industrial and political leaders, not working people and community activists. (Check back to the discussion in Unit 7 about the importance of Canadian versus American and British textbooks, in studying Canadian economic development from the perspective of Canada.) It's through structural monopolies of knowledge that some concepts of what's central and what's marginal are reinforced from one generation of learners to the next.

Structural monopolies are effected by where information is stored and how it is structured, packaged and distributed. A monopoly is more likely to emerge where information is concentrated in a few central storage sites and distributed over a wide receiving area than where information sources are themselves widely distributed among the receiving population. There are also structures within the knowledge structures themselves, as the example of bibliographic databases clearly illustrates. In a world of burgeoning information, technologies for sorting and categorizing information, and for searching intelligently through it, have become increasingly important. Companies in this new field of bibliographic databases and search-engine software could become a new source of structural monopolies of knowledge.

The potential for monopoly was apparent from an early date, in the rise to prominence of two bibliographic database companies, Mead Data General and Dialog, which is owned by the newspaper chain Knight Ridder. By 1984, these two companies accounted for 82 percent of the revenue generated by the on-line bibliographic searching business. Canada's newspaper chain, Thomson Corporation, has also become a major player both in bibliographic databases and in specialized software for information searching. In 1995, Thomson was selling some 270 on-line services and 6,540 software products. Its information-services division grossed more than $3 billion US in 1994 (Schachter, 1995:36).

Apart from the monopoly suggested in the scale of these operations, there's the potential for monopolizing knowledge in how searches are steered. This happens, most obviously, in the packaging and storage of information inside these databases. And it happens both in the choice of what to include or leave out of the reference base and in the categories in which various information is indexed.

An Australian study found that the biggest "international" databases often didn't index all the Australian journals. In fact, many database suppliers follow a tiered system of indexing, with a core set of journals (including the *New England Journal of Medicine* in medicine) indexed to the full, a second tier where articles are indexed selectively, and a third where only minimal indexing is done. Researchers aren't in a position to know readily the biases at work in this structuring process, nor to check them out since the database suppliers are often half a world away. As a clinical psychologist wrote in the journal, *On-line*, "I also don't know where my inadequacies end and [those of] the databases begin. In other words, I'm not sure every article is indexed to its fullest potential." (Menzies, 1993:796)

3)Cultural Monopolies of Knowledge

The cultural aspect of monopolies of knowledge has a lot to do with why that psychologist is dependent on these international databases. Increasingly, such people participate in international discourses, or academic discussions, which are built on constant reference to previously published and discussed material.

Today, monopolies of knowledge operate culturally in these vast systems of structured, objectified and commoditized knowledge because of our society's widespread orientation to experts and objectified expert knowledge. In the Middle Ages, when the church held a monopoly of knowledge and public perception, the cultural monopoly operated through that society's orientation to religious explanations and related knowledge as authoritative. In Harold Innis' view, cultural monopolies of knowledge represented the most fundamental form of social power, because they amounted to the power to determine what reality was. In the Middle Ages, the designated authorities of the church had the power to pronounce this the work of God and that the work of the devil. Today, that power is distributed through the various hierarchies associated with the production and distribution of official public knowledge as well as popular knowledge, pronouncing this as actionable policy and that as public opinion.

Monopolies of knowledge operate culturally along three dimensions: 1) through the things thought about, for example, "economic growth" as a measure of societal well being; 2) through the things thought with, such as statistics and the official experts and institutions producing them, and textbooks, newspapers and, now, bibliographic databases publishing them; 3) through the communities of interest involved, that is, credentialed academics for official knowledge and media producers for public and popular knowledge and perception (Carey, 1975:35).

The idea of a cultural monopoly of knowledge relates back to Ursula Franklin's idea about how "constructed realities" of the media have eclipsed the vernacular realities of people in local communities. It also harks back to George Grant and his ideas of people's dependence on technique and technology. His phrase "technique is ourselves" suggests that in matters of public decision making, technical rationality has gained a cultural monopoly as the only real way of thinking and arriving at a public truth. People don't speak for themselves. Experts speak for them. And all these ideas shed light on the concept of "manufacturing consent" popularized by Edward Herman and Noam Chomsky.

PUTTING THE CONCEPTS TOGETHER In practice, all three aspects of monopolies of knowledge work together. The physical monopoly of speed and pace conferred through satellite communication has helped create a whole new standard in news making. The things thought about are the steady supply of sights and sounds for 30-second news clips and 20-second sound bites. The things thought with are the globally transmitted images. The communities of interest are those news agencies, such as CNN, which can deliver this staple of the news.

The phenomenon of Hollywood movies, and how central they are to the landscape of shared myths and legends, also illustrates this synergy. First, the cultural monopoly of knowledge operates through the brand-name stars, the high-voltage drama and the glitzy special effects of Hollywood movies, plus the various agents (including talk-show hosts) who promote the latest Hollywood releases and bring them to the public's attention. This is reinforced by the physical monopoly associated with the rapid deployment of Hollywood films through the North American circuit of theatres, where first-run movies command the bulk of audiences, and revenues. A fast-forward loop is created here, with the promotion of "the latest" hot film generating instant box-office revenues, and rapid box-office turnover, making room for the next big hit. Thus too, the big-budget (glitzy, hot) Hollywood films that can quickly draw a broad mass audience to fill the large-scale film-distribution system will maintain their monopoly on public perception as the movies everyone is talking about. By contrast, most movies that don't conform to these commercial standards either won't draw a mass audience or won't do it within the fast turnover standard set by the chains. They will tend to be excluded, not by a conspiracy of exclusion but by the monopoly dynamics built into the structures and operating principles.

BREAKING MONOPOLIES OF KNOWLEDGE As the discussion in Unit 8 made clear, Canadian film making does exist. The monopolies haven't shut Canadian film makers out completely, although many have turned their backs on the industrial production and distribution model. They have, instead, confronted the cultural monopoly that would define culture solely as consumption, and have embraced the more participative approach that sees culture as communication. They rely on non-commercial production facilities such as video and film-making cooperatives. Strategically, too, many deliberately

keep their production budgets low. By operating more on a cost-recovery basis than a profit-maximization one, these film makers also avoid some of the costly risks associated with big-budget promotions to attract a mass audience of anonymous consumers. The lower risk means they can take their time to cultivate an audience, through film festivals and independent film exhibitors.

The *Sun* printing plant, Ottawa

Still the question remains: have these film makers actually broken the cultural monopoly that defines good movies in Hollywood terms of reference, as readily consumable entertainment? Have successive generations of Canadian (and Australian, African, Russian, German, Dutch, Japanese, etc.) filmmakers succeeded in redefining film making standards along more pluralistic lines? And is a craft-scale marginal existence enough?

Harold Innis' interest in breaking monopolies of knowledge and perception had nothing to do with championing any particular interest group's cause nor championing any particular ideology. His approach, like Ursula Franklin's, was an intensely pragmatic one. He was interested in promoting stability and peace in society. He thought this was best preserved by promoting multiple centres of knowledge and by promoting a balance of communication media and of interests associated with different media. He admired the society of Ancient Greece because the tendency for monopolies of knowledge to develop around written texts was offset by the Greeks' strong oral tradition.

Ursula Franklin didn't talk about monopolies of knowledge as such, but they are implied in her discussion of "experts" dominating the process of public planning. To counter this, she recommends a discourse of public planning centred on people and human experience where people are no longer the consumers of expert-designed plans, but participants.

The 1977 Berger Inquiry into the MacKenzie Valley pipeline illustrates many of both Franklin's and Innis' points. The inquiry was set up to investigate whether opening up the Northwest Territories to major oil and gas development was beneficial, not just as a general idea, nor just for the consortium of petroleum companies that wanted to build the pipeline. The question was whether it was beneficial for the native population and the wildlife and land base of the MacKenzie Valley on which they'd depended to survive since the beginning of time. Given monopolies of knowledge, the thrust of the "research" around the inquiry was done by "experts." The terms of reference used by these experts were predominantly economic ones — testing the viability of the local native economy and whether a pipeline was needed to boost it with local employment opportunities. The related communities of interest were the pipeline companies and the Department of Indian Affairs and Northern Development, which traditionally spoke for native and northern concerns.

Berger offset these monopolies of knowledge with several innovative moves. 1) He provided research money to native groups so they could create their own "expert" knowledge and could speak for themselves; 2) He held hearings throughout the north, and across southern Canada too, so that people could tell their own stories in their own terms; 3) He took his time, giving everyone a chance to speak. No one was cut off. There was no tight time line that favoured those who could get their views and their knowledge delivered fastest.

Not surprisingly, the economists who did the research for the Indian Brotherhood of the Northwest Territories used different terms of reference when calculating the viability of the northern native economy. While the economists employed by the gas companies, and by the federal government, followed the classical mainstream terms, in which anything that didn't have a market or cash value didn't count, the native group's economists used terms that made sense of the Indians' reality as they lived it. And so, the food value of the animals skinned for the fur trade was calculated as value, as were the fish, berries and other foods harvested strictly for food (Usher, 1989:8-13). And since the family is the basic economic unit in northern native society, not the individual acting alone, one trapping license was valued as supporting a whole family.

The knowledge and reality portrayed by the mainstream commerce-oriented economists wasn't deliberately misleading. However, because of the monopolies of knowledge built into the tools they were using and the world view they were operating from, they simply missed huge chunks of the northern native reality (Berger, 1977:8). As a result, they misrepresented and underrepresented that reality.

A truer picture of that reality only emerged because of Berger's initiatives to offset the systemic biases. His final report combined personal stories of native elders speaking their truth with the economic facts, and the discrepancy between the northern native and southern business representations of them.

NEW WORLD INFORMATION ORDER The Berger Inquiry broke monopolies of knowledge around what development and economy was understood to be in the North of Canada. The efforts to establish a New World Information Order have been an attempt to break such monopolies around the world. The project was inspired by the huge disparities in communication and media technology between the so-called developed and lesser and undeveloped world. By the late 1970s, 80 transnational corporations controlled 75 percent of the international communication market, including everything from infrastructure to tools and content, ranging from films to television and news. It represented such an intense penetration of information and cultural images, sponsored by American advertising companies pushing American or look-alike branch-plant products, that as Cees Hamelink noted (Hamelink, 1983:2) starving children in Brazil beg for Barbie dolls as well as food.

> "[T]he impressive variety of the world's cultural systems is waning due to a process of 'cultural synchronization' that is without precedent. It appears that public recognition of cultural diversity is kept alive only on the folkloric level when traditional ceremonies, flags and dress adorn international gatherings." (Hamelink, 1983:4)

The tension over cultural autonomy and communication technology was evident in the founding constitution of the United Nations Educational, Scientific and Cultural Organization (UNESCO) in 1946 when it stressed the need to use communication technology to improve mutual understanding among nations. Although the United States pushed hard for a "free flow of information" as the meaning of information freedom, by 1972, that had been modified to "a free and balanced information flow."

Through the early '70s there was a concerted effort from non-aligned countries in Africa and elsewhere to link the new communication order with the new economic world order. This shows an early recognition of how important communication technology was becoming for the fundamentals of political economy. (This was discussed in Unit 5 and will be touched on again in Unit 10.)

At their 1973 meeting in Algiers, the non-aligned countries agreed that "developing countries should take concerted action to reorganize existing communication channels which are a legacy from the colonial past." The 1976 meeting in Tunis of the non-aligned countries called for the "emancipation of the mass media in Non-aligned countries." It also called for a mutual fund to be established to foster the development of mass media in non-aligned countries under local national control. Subsequently, the General Conference of UNESCO debated the Tunis resolution, pleading support for third-world countries wanting to build their own information infrastructures, and gave it nearly unanimous acceptance. Support grew, including even from the *Washington Post*, which commented that "it must be galling to Third World people to see their newspapers, films, TV shows ... promoting consumer and value models of slender relevance to their own societies." (Hamelink, 1983:60)

In 1978, the 33rd session of the United Nations General Assembly adopted a resolution affirming "the need to establish a new, more just and more effective world information and communication order intended to strengthen international peace and understanding."

The International Commission for the Study of Communication Problems published the famous MacBride Report in 1980, full of good principles though somewhat lacking in plans for action. A workshop for third-world communication researchers in the Hague articulated the problem as the monopoly structures of existing communication media, whose "verticalism and authoritarianism," they felt should be replaced by "democratization, genuine public access and social participation."

The rhetoric continued for some time. However, in Hamelink's analysis, the original vision of social and structural change had been remoulded by the 21st General Conference of UNESCO in Belgrade in October 1980. There, delegates supported a program for the general improvement of communication infrastructures in third-world countries. The rhetoric and principles had remained the same. But the United States representative to the UNESCO, John Reinhardt, had introduced the idea that these goals could best be achieved by transferring American technology to third-world countries to improve their powers of communication. As Hamelink said, the crucial political questions about control over the structures of production, distribution and marketing in international communication were pushed out of the picture.

"The new world information and communication order could very well turn out to be the world order of the transnational corporations, the *corporate village*, but now with international political blessing." (Hamelink, 1983:70) [emphasis added]

COMMENTARY ON SUPPLEMENTARY READINGS

James Carey, "Canadian Communication Theory: Extensions and Interpretations of Harold Innis."

This is a wonderful, though dense, essay. It reiterates a lot of points about the bias of communication made in earlier units, and also provides a detailed description of monopolies of knowledge. Note the following important points:

* Monopolies of knowledge can grow most quickly in cultural climates pretending to articulate THE universal truth.

* Societies exist in time and space. These dimensions are reciprocally related through different media of communication. Spatially oriented communication is geared to fast, long-distance communication. Time-oriented communication is slower and geared to shorter distances: local, personal and intimate communication.

* A high-communication policy (in societies emphasizing space-oriented communication) will extend language over vast distances, yet drain it of its emotive richness and complexity, and therefore of its ability to serve the time interests of memory and tradition.

* Long-distance communication also creates new relations of long-distance power and control, which blunts the effective capacity of local and proximate relations. These relations create special classes of readers, viewers and other communication receivers/consumers, with little chance of communication between themselves.

* A high communication policy will strengthen relations between centres and margins of social space (sources of knowledge and receivers), while weakening communication within that space.

* As communication improves in speed and technical efficiency and is reduced in cost, so the tendency is to centralize authority and decision making, while spreading out the reach of that authority, through markets or administrative structures (of empires and corporations).

* Culture, as seen in relation to the communication which supports it, can be therefore understood as the "forms of thought" and the "models constructed out of symbols" that "serve to contain and guide human action." As such, thought is essentially public because it derives from these shared frames of reference and "significant symbols."

* Changes in communication technology alter culture by changing the things thought about (land as real estate, economy as market activity); the things thought with (the price system and the whole language of commerce); and the patterns of community. Space-biased communication creates "communities in space" such as national consumer and business associations.

* In short, the medium is the message: "structures of consciousness parallel structures of communication."

* A bias of communication can harden into a monopoly when certain groups come to control the form or medium of communication and to identity their interests priestly (time) or political (space) with it.

* Physically, a monopoly of knowledge is created when information can be made to move at unequal speeds, so what is future to one person is present to another.

* Structurally, a monopoly of knowledge relates to the centralization or decentralization of knowledge, and where it is stored. It creates a situation of knowledgeable elites at the centres of knowledge production and ignorant masses. In other words, "we keep waiting to be informed, to be educated, but lose the capacity to produce knowledge for ourselves in decentralized communities of understanding."

* Cultural monopolies of knowledge apply at the level of world view and the mental maps subtly imposed through a communication medium, particularly if it is structured. Hence, computer programmers don't want to monopolize data. What's important is to perpetuate the cultural reliance, or monopoly, on the databased approach to public thought and problem solving that keeps their profession and their technology so central to contemporary public life.

* Universities, according to Innis, should serve as society's "loyal opposition," countering the dominant values and biases in the more political and economic institutions of society. Instead, he sees the university being drawn into a new role of support for those institutions.

* Communication can be seen as the basic staple in the growth of empire.

* Innis embraced the "tragic" poetics of dialectics, which recognized the limitations of human action, but nevertheless championed the power of countervailing influences. Innis' dialectics were time and space, church and empire, stability and change, written and oral traditions, Roman and Common law, force and moral sanction.

QUESTIONS FOR DISCUSSION

This brings us to the end of Module III, which took a broadly historical look at the history of communication in culture. Test your comprehension of the concepts you've learned in this chapter by applying them to what you learned in Chapters 7 and 8.

1) How are the structures of mass-circulation newspapers conducive to creating monopolies of knowledge?
2) Why is public ownership in the media important in breaking monopolies of public perception and opinion?
3) How did the Berger Inquiry break monopolies of knowledge in policy decision making re. Canada's far north?

SOURCES AND FURTHER READINGS

Berger, Thomas, 1977. *Northern Frontier, Northern Homeland: The Report of the MacKenzie Valley Pipeline Inquiry*. Vol. 2. Ottawa: Supply and Services Canada.

Carey, James, 1975. "Canadian Communication Theory: Extensions and Interpretations of Harold Innis," in *Studies in Canadian Communications*. Robinson, G.J. and Theall, D.F., eds. Montreal: McGill Studies in Communications.

Hamelink, Cees, 1983. *Cultural Autonomy in Global Communications*. New York: Longmans.

Innis, Harold, 1984. *The Bias of Communication*. Toronto: University of Toronto Press.

McLuhan, Marshall, 1964. *Understanding Media: The Extensions of Man*. New York: Mentor.

Menzies, Heather, 1993. "Information Gathering and Confidentiality: Databases, Monopolies of Knowledge and the Right to be Informed," in *Human Rights in the Twenty-first Century: A Global Challenge*. Mahoney, K.E. and Mahoney, P., eds. Martinus-Nijhoff Publishers.

Schachter, Harry, 1995. "Information Overlord," *Canadian Business* (November).

Splichal, Slavko and Wasko, Janet, eds., 1993. *Communication and Democracy*. Norwood, NJ: Ablex.

Usher, Peter, 1989. *Towards a Strategy for Supporting the Domestic Economy of the Northwest Territories*. Yellowknife, NWT: Clerk of the Legislative Assembly.

MODULE IV

SUMMING UP

The journey of this text, and the course it might be part of, is nearly over. We began with the shipping lines of the Hudson's Bay Company. We're ending here with the satellite links of the global information society. In between we've picked up some valuable lessons in how technologies are constructed out of values and world views as well as large-scale or small-scale material structures and social organizations. There have also been lessons in how particularly large-scale capital-intensive technologies can, in turn, strongly determine the lines of a whole country's development, and keep extending those lines from one generation of technology to another. We've also seen how large-scale technological infrastructures, particularly in transportation and communication, can shape not only a society's political economy but also its sense of identity.

In Unit 10 we will apply all those lessons in considering the possibilities for Canada and for people inside the fully realized sensorium of global communication networks. The unit will look at the basic building blocks of the global village, and the alternative models for the village suggested in the Internet versus the Information Highway. It will also consider the major players involved in the various converging technologies and what these convergences suggest. It ends with a panel discussion on the possibilities for culture and identity in this new environment.

Unit 11 concludes the discussion through a more direct focus on the values and world view informing choices and uses of technology. While women have featured prominently throughout this course, we'll specifically take a woman-centred or feminist perspective here to highlight what could be called a "monoculture" of thinking which sees everything from economy to development and even the solution of personal and social problems through a technology-centred lens. It will return us to the values discussion of Unit 3, and ask whether it's possible to realize a just, reciprocal ecological world order based not on the values of economic growth and development, but on the values of peaceful co-existence and survival.

Unit 12 is a straightforward review. The video features excerpts from the preceding units, while chapter 12 reviews the key themes and concepts.

OBJECTIVES

At the end of this module, you will be able to see beyond the surface of the converging communication universe, and critically assess the shift from a world of nation states and local cultures to that of a global village. You will be able to ask whether the global village is sustainable, and specifically whether it's structured to sustain Canadian culture and human diversity.

CHAPTER 10

IMAGINING CANADA IN THE GLOBAL VILLAGE

OVERVIEW

This unit takes you inside the global village — that is, the global digital networks that are pulling more and more aspects of people's lives into its cybernetic space. It also brings home some fundamental questions about democracy and social justice, and the bias of communication. When the social spaces in which people move to make a living, to seek out friends, to get an education and a line of credit are spaces created through the converged multi-media networks, there's more at stake than whose voice is heard and whose stories are excluded. Questions of access turn into urgent questions of meaningful participation in the new society.

The chapter begins with the building blocks of the emerging information society, the emerging global village. It will describe the various media involved in the current convergence into multimedia. It will also describe some of the main corporate players involved, such as Microsoft in information systems and software, and Rogers and Bell in cable television and telephones. Then it will set this discussion in the critical frame of the two models of communication discussed in the previous modules: the commodity-transmission model and the social-bonding model. It will also point out how these two models fit the two configurations of global information networks: the Information Highway and the Internet.

The global village could be a global extension of diverse local communities, or it could be a local extension of a global monoculture. It all depends on the values built into the material structures and related organizational, management and regulatory structures involved.

The video portion of the unit ends with a panel discussion, including three communication scholars and an industry executive, where such questions will be explored in sometimes heated detail.

OBJECTIVES

The goal of this unit is to help you think critically about the unfolding information society. At the end of it, you should be able to answer the following questions:

1) What model of communication does the Information Highway metaphor fit, and why?
2) What model does the Internet fit, and why is the fit a less than perfect one?

THERE ARE MANY CRITICAL QUESTIONS around the global village of instant global connectivity. For example, who is building it? Who is invited to enter, and on what terms? And will it support us all, not just with "jobs" in the industrial meaning of work, but with opportunities to make a place for ourselves and to live at peace with each other? Will it be built on the principles of social justice, reciprocity and equity, the building blocks of democracy and peace? Or will it be built on the narrower principles of commerce: with access, mobility and involvement limited largely to those with the ability to pay? Some of the answers lie in the building-block technologies, in the corporate players involved and in the models of communication they're mostly applying, and the role of the state backing one, the other or both.

BUILDING-BLOCK TECHNOLOGIES Although much of the hype about convergence centres on broadcasting and how television is merging with telephones and computers, the core convergence came before that, between computers and telecommunications.

1) Computer-Communication

This convergence dates back to the invention of the microchip in 1972. It put computer power into communication devices, opening the world to intelligent switching systems and distributed data processing. Computers, and chips, are the key to the integration of various communication tools, from satellites to fibre-optic cable and copper phone lines, and the creation of intelligent interactive systems. Business was the first to tap the scope of these systems, particularly businesses in the financial-information sector: banks, insurance companies, and brokerage houses. One could say, in fact, that the global village first appeared in the form of global, financial information systems, symbolized locally by the banking kiosk. The global computer-communication networks permitting international flows of financial capital was the first step in the transformation of national economies into a global digital systems economy, as discussed in Unit 5.

They also set the stage for a new cybernetic environment not just for the financing of economies, but for their operation as well. This environment broke the bonds of natural space (or place) and even natural time, as it permitted 24-hour investment and trading, and created new material realities within the frame of its media space, including multi-media communication.

2) Television/cable and Digital Communication

This convergence is significant in many ways. First, it allows cable companies to provide telephone services, and telephone companies to become broadcasters. It also signals a transformation of mass-market broadcasting into customized multiple-choice distribution. With computer smarts built into the relevant equipment, such as telephones or cable, conventional broadcasting can be customized for "on-demand" programs, movies and other information products. The smart television, or cable black box, will offer a range of digital services, everything from tele-shopping via specialized home-shopping channels, to tele-learning. The continuing convergence is enlarging the range of information goods and services that can be channelled down the cable/telephone pipeline, opening the possibility of one-stop shopping and service for a dizzying range of information goods and services.

3) Publishing

As information is digitized, the scope for convergence rises accordingly. Since the 1980s, newspapers have had digital back issues available on-line. They've also developed these into indexed and cross-referenced databases and developed software tools for navigating to and through them. Some newspaper companies, such as Knight Ridder in the US and Thomson in Canada, have also invested in bibliographic database publishing and related searching and organizing software. Some of these are available on cable, others through the Internet. With computers and communications, publishing is moving into a host of different genres or formats, including CD Roms (with text, audio, video and graphics integrated on a single disk) which can be used as a reference tool or in conjunction with video-conferencing.

4) Tele-services

Convergence here has created a new business associated with marketing and market transactions. The new digital services range from banking to hotel and airline reservations, to government employment services and 1-800 back-up to cable-based shopping. Equally, the scope for tele-services extends through a range of public services, including tele-medicine. Tele-medicine can range from the exotic of remote-control robotocized surgery to remote diagnostics where data from diagnostic equipment — say, Xray images — is relayed from a remote community to a large urban centre where a specialist can analyze the data and advise the local medical people on diagnosis and treatment.

5) Interactive Games

Interactive games marry graphics with computers. Increasingly these games can be accessed through the Internet's global communication networks. With some games, such as multi-user dungeons (MUDs), they can be changed through on-line interaction. Now, many aspects of these play-oriented innovations are being applied elsewhere: the graphics language has become almost a new universal language in global communications on the World Wide Web (WWW). And the software supporting interactivity is being applied to a number of other venues, such as interactive shopping. The habits formed from playing interactive games also prepare people nicely to participate in the world virtually, and in isolation from others, perhaps for long periods of time.

But the full dynamism of the converging technologies isn't in the technologies themselves. It's in the new environment they're creating as they converge. To identify the choice paths and the design options that are being considered, or not, in shaping this environment, it's useful to look at the key players involved.

CONVERGING COMPANIES There are two groups of players to consider: those providing the various communication systems and services; and those providing the infrastructure. At the level of infrastructure, which is the equivalent of the rail lines and switching yards of a railway system or the lines and switchboards of a telephone system, the previously public or publicly regulated networking infrastructures are largely being replaced with private-sector control and regulation. In Canada, a consortium of mostly private-sector institutions centred on telephone-industry interests (CANARIE) has taken over the management of the Canadian backbone of the global network of communication networks known as the Internet, CA*net. With 50 percent funding from the federal government, the consortium had a mandate to upgrade that infrastructure to handle multi-media at accelerated speeds. While membership expanded through the '90s to include most Canadian universities and research institutes, its founding members, who drafted the original business plan and set the bylaws, were strongly business-centred. They included Bell, Unitel, Northern Telecom, Stentor Resource Centre, IBM Canada, Hewlett Packard, Newbridge and Canada Trust (Menzies, 1994:25).

Buttressing this private-sector dominance, the policy-making process has been largely left to the Information Highway Advisory Council, with over 50 percent of its membership tied to business interests. In its 1995 report, the council's first recommendations were all geared to letting the private sector and "market demand" govern the development path of the infrastructure (see box).

> Rec. 1.1. "The federal government should recognize the urgent need to deal with the regulatory framework and initiate action to remove barriers and implement safeguards, thereby ensuring the right environment for competitive development."
> Rec. 1.2 "Highway network and new infrastructure should be left to the private sector, and the risks and rewards of the investment should accrue to the shareholders."
> Rec. 1.3 "The provision of the Information Highway facilities across the nation must be driven by existing or potential market demand." (Industry Canada, 1995:92)

In addition to the infrastructure, there are the multi-media conglomerates offering systems, services and multi-media content. Rogers

Communication is one of the Canadian conglomerates involved. In 1994, Rogers took over Maclean Hunter, which owns two of Canada's biggest magazines, *Maclean's* and *Chatelaine*, plus 62 other magazines, publishes five newspapers including the *Financial Post*, and also runs 21 radio stations and one TV station across the country. Rogers is the largest cable company in Canada, and is therefore well poised to deliver all kinds of multi-media product to subscribers, including material originally prepared for newspaper and magazine publication. In Quebec, a provincial cable company, Videotron announced a multi-media joint venture involving Hydro-Quebec, Loto-Quebec, Canada Post, the National Bank and the Hearst newspaper chain (Menzies, 1994:18).

Some of the largest joint ventures and multi-media mergers have involved American companies: Microsoft has formed an alliance with General Instruments, which makes TV converters; and another with Tele-Communications, the largest cable company in the US.

Time-Warner has merged with Turner Broadcasting, which controls CNN and also a film distribution company, Fine Line Features, of New Line Cinema (Johnson, 1996:72).

Another interesting case of convergence involves electric-power companies, with General Electric taking over NBC and Westinghouse Electric bidding $7.3 billion for CBS. Disney Corporation added the ABC television network to its already bulging multi-media portfolio which includes books, videos, Disney World entertainment parks and Miramax Films (McMurdy, 1995:32). Finally, the cable giant Viacom has acquired Paramount Communication, which also controls the Famous Players theatre chain.

With each of these conglomerates worth billions of dollars, it sets a monopoly-scale standard for effective participation in this new environment.

Another way of looking at convergence is between the levels on which communication systems operate: carrier and content, or message sender and receiver, or system/service supplier and end user. Within these pairings, it's then useful to trace the social relations and the relative power or clout involved in either side. For example, end users of televisions, telephones and computers are more numerous than the suppliers. But the latter are organized into large corporate conglomerates, whereas the users are not. This might become a more pressing social issue as more end users start working from home, using their digital equipment as work environments and work tools.

On the supplier side, convergence of multi-media technology is collapsing the distinctions between infrastructure, systems, services and other "content." Furthermore, deregulation is permitting corporate integration among these different levels. The phone and cable companies building and operating the infrastructures could soon be supplying a range of information systems and services, from at-home banking to software support for home offices, plus a range of learning materials and entertainment content. Many of these services were either available commercially in the mid-1990s or were being field-tested.

The scope for monopoly scale is enormous, especially as the convergence starts collapsing the boundaries between home and work, and between previously separate institutions such as school, library, museum, arcade, mall and theme park.

James Carey, Columbia University. (Stephen Wormarski)

DESIGN OPTIONS FOR THE GLOBAL VILLAGE So far, we've discussed the building blocks and some of the major corporate interests behind the construction of the global village. We can now go deeper and consider what values and social priorities are being designed and wired into this village, this new digital environment in which more and more of us are spending more of our lives.

It's useful to revisit Innis' insights about the bias of communication in a society revealing the values bias of the society itself. He argued that in the modern commercial era, the bias of communication was toward fast, distance-spanning media of transportation and communication because these are useful to convey new raw materials to market, and to expand the market geographically for distributing more finished products. The bias of the modern era was toward controlling space, by turning it into commodity markets. This bias was in turn served by fast, distance-spanning media: sailing ships in the mercantile phase of commercialism; railways and steamships in the industrial era and, latterly, satellites, airplanes and global digital networks in today's post-industrial era.

Furthermore, as James Carey noted (see Unit 7), fast, long-distance communication systems have a tendency to consolidate authority in a few centres, create unequal relations between centre and margin, and blunt the capacity for intimate, local relations and for relations from one marginal point to another.

Yet various groups, from adult education to national liberation movements, women's groups and environmentalists, have seized various new, fast, distance-spanning media and tried to retool them to reflect their own values — values more closely associated with Innis' conception of the time bias: time as continuity, tradition, conservation and community (see box).

It is important not to ascribe too much determinism to the technology itself. Technology is a social and political construct, and can be designed differently to embody different social and political values. The Internet and the Information Highway are good examples of this.

FARM RADIO FORUM

The Farm Radio Forum was an exercise in community-communication jointly sponsored by the Canadian Association of Adult Education, the Canadian Federation of Agriculture and the CBC. Launched in 1941 as a way for people to come to grips with a new world war following the 1930s Depression, it adopted a four-step formula: read, listen, discuss and act. First, discussion materials were mailed out to participating farmer groups. Then "listening groups" (farm families gathering in each others' homes) would listen to a lecture or discussion broadcast on the radio. They would then discuss the issue of the week, and come up with their own suggestions for action. These would be forwarded to the forum office, and aired in subsequent broadcasts, thus completing the cycle of communication with shared reciprocity. Many university extension departments became involved, cultivating and supporting rural participation. Several important civic initiatives emerged from the discussions, including co-operative medical services, co-operative buying clubs and stores, rural electrification and community centres. The forum continued for over a decade, and served as a model for at least 44 other countries.

As one Saskatchewan participant put it: "There was a real sense that this was our community."

(Cruikshank and Faris, 1994:30)

INTERNET AND INFORMATION HIGHWAY

The term "information highway" was coined by US vice-president Al Gore in 1993 when he introduced his $2-billion-a-year National Information Infrastructure Program. As discussed in Chapter 5, Gore's agenda had a strong business orientation. However, most of the hype surrounding the information highway, both in the US and Canada, concentrated on the potential for distributing entertainment and commercial services. The highway metaphor is strongly associated with a commercial use of digital communication and the multimedia conglomerates identified with it. It's a commercial, supplier model, which sees end users as consumers, and as professionals and paid workers too.

By contrast, the Internet is more of an end-user model. It also sees users as active participants in the information environment, applying the technology holistically. It's worth remembering at the outset, though, that the Internet was created by a strongly space-biased institution: the US Department of Defense. But its communication-control network was strategically designed (in 1969) as a self-governing collection of information nodes, rather than a centrally controlled system, so that the network could withstand the destruction of any particular site. This decentred design feature has been a key to its growth along non-space-biased dimensions. Participating research scientists broke out of their institutional boundaries. They began communicating horizontally with colleagues, friends and kindred spirits in various causes, such as the environment. These people in turn reached out to others. And so it went, to the point that Internet has entered popular mythology as a wild and wonderful community of communities, with no one in control, and everyone free to use it as they see fit. It is also known for its macho hacker individualism and a hectoring, sometimes bullying, tone, with sexual harassment as a recurring subtext for women. The WELL out of San Francisco was started by the publishers of the *Whole Earth Catalogue*, and is considered by some to be the prototype for community freenets. It's also part of a larger network of networks, called the Association for Progressive Computing, with nodes in Canada (the Web, in Toronto), England (GreenNet, in London), Scandinavia, the US, Nicaragua (niconet) and Brazil (alternex).

Community nets (formerly called freenets) represent a fascinating mini-renaissance in community communications. Defined by Carleton University's Jay Weston as community-based not-for-profit computer information networks, community nets also represent some of the first efforts to move beyond simply appropriating existing network technology. Participants are actually designing their own systems around local community-communications goals and values. By 1995, there were 14 freenets in Canada, and dozens more in the US, New Zealand and Germany, with the numbers growing exponentially. In Ottawa, the National Capital Freenet, launched in 1992, had more than 27,000 registered users by 1995, including over 100 local and national organizations ranging from the Ottawa Psychiatric Survivors Alliance, the La Leche League, the Saw Video Co-op, the Canadian Environmental Network, plus various news services and discussion fora on economic development.

All in all, they tend to fit what James Carey has defined as a community-building "ritual" model of communication, as compared to the dominant "transmission" model of communication (Carey, 1989:15). While the transmission model is concerned with moving as much information as fast and efficiently as possible, the ritual model views communication through the more spiritual lens of social bonding and social relationships. The former is geared to the business and economics of transporting commodities, and operates largely through the private sector. The latter is geared to community building and culture, which are prime concerns of the community networks. The transmission model is booming ahead under the Information Highway banner and the multi-media conglomerates carrying it. The latter requires public-sector support.

Community-building Model	Transmission Model
* organic	* mechanical
* comm. as process & social relations	* comm. as product
* comm. as conversation	* comm. as transaction
* ecological/growth model of comm.	* ec./production model of comm.
* values involvement	* values speed and turnover
* time-oriented (spiritual)	* space-oriented (material)
* non-commercial (needs public support/regulation)	* commercial (champions market regulation)
* extension of grounded community	* creates communities of space

Community nets, however, are all subsidized services. In Ottawa, for instance, the freenet piggybacks on the computer system of Carleton University. In Toronto, Rogers Cable (Rogers Communication) subsidized the launch of a community net there through donations of equipment and space worth an estimated $7,000 a month. In the US, the Corporation for Public Broadcasting in partnership with US West awarded $1.4 million to support 12 community networking projects in the early '90s. These initiatives, seen within the larger context of government downsizing and public-spending cuts plus the privatization of the Internet infrastructure, would suggest that they're all at risk of being enclosed by the larger infrastructures on which they depend. And many of these service providers — Rogers Communication for example — are prime exemplars of the transmission model of communication. Public funding and policy support are essential to sustain this model in a social environment dominated by commercial interests, and to prevent it stalling in a state of under-development like community-access cable (see Unit 8).

CRITICAL DESIGN QUESTIONS

As mentioned in Unit 1, this course is a journey of questions about what it is to be Canadian and even what it means to be human inside the 500-channel universe, inside the global village.

We've established that the global village is a computerized communication network, with a range of multi-media appliances, tools, products and services available throughout it. We've established that it embodies the space bias in the root communication technologies involved, in the founding institutional players (including the US Defense Department) and in what seems to be the dominant communication model informing the design and running of this new environment.

However, we've also found evidence of a different design at work that would run the global village as an inclusive community of diverse communities. This is the community-building, social-bonding and even "ecological" model associated with the groups that have consciously appropriated the Internet and turned it into a tool for conversation, as well as a bonding mechanism for providing solidarity between groups that have been traditionally excluded from the dominant media systems: community groups, environmental groups, women, native groups, labour and refugee-support groups and social-justice groups. (The idea of an "ecological" model of communication is discussed further in Unit 11.) Almost exclusively, these groups are operating at the first level of communication mentioned above. They are the end-user groups, and though they are seldom mentioned as institutional players in discussions about the information society, they represent a powerful potential force.

In the late 1990s, the development both of this new technology and of the post-industrial paradigm of social organization were still in the enterprise-growth stage, although the multi-media mergers suggested that the institutionalization phase was beginning. Investment requirements and related systems were becoming rigid.

In this period, the end-user groups, plus the content group of writers, film makers and other artists were engaged in a struggle for control, or even survival, with the large-scale corporate interests associated with the transmission model and the information highway. These are the carriers, the infrastructure, systems and service suppliers. In the late 1990s, these groups were also becoming more organized, and more politically active.

The kind of grassroots, community-based organizing that helped to launch public radio in Canada in the 1930s seems to be necessary (see Unit 8). From what previous experience with communication infrastructure and policy has taught us (consider Community-Access Cable in Unit 8) a parallel public system, or multi-media communication space, is also needed, as are design principles supporting such time-related values as:

1) people in communication over machines in communication;

2) reciprocity in two-way communication, not one-way distribution with multiple-choice feedback options;

3) open, democratic systems, not closed proprietary systems;

4) a policy commitment to a mixed-model approach to communication.

5) cyber communities as an extension of grounded face-to-face communities, and both accountable to them and sustained by oral communication within them.

As the panel discussion on the video made clear, the issues are tied in with the future of democracy and diversity. They're also intimately tied to human autonomy and privacy, and the capacity of people to come together in communities other than consumer and professional groups.

COMMENTARY ON SUPPLEMENTARY READINGS

1) Heather Menzies, *Whose Brave New World? The Information Highway and the New Economy*, pp. 143-55.

The reading makes the following points:

* Historically, people's work environment, as well as the environments where they learnt and shopped, socialized and relaxed, was locally controlled, although often with varying degrees of remote control through bureaucratic rules and boss's orders. There was some scope for face-to-face negotiation and working something out. However, with computerized instructions, access protocols, and so on constituting the new environment for work and for getting work, the scope for local and personal control is severely reduced. Who programs and controls that programmed environment therefore becomes very important.

* Real control lies beyond the end-user level, at the level of systems services, operating systems and infrastructure.

* The transmission model views communication as a modified form of transportation. The emphasis is on product delivery, and keeping the transmission lines full.

* The bias is toward the expansion of markets and military or commercial empires.

* The ritual or communitarian model of communication encourages reciprocity and a diffusion of control among users.

* Because communication here is not geared to making money, though it might still cost money, it's generally supported by costless technologies, subsidized technologies or regulated media systems. Here, time isn't and cannot be equated to money.

* Would-be practitioners of this model of communication, associated with many of the grassroots democratic and community-building projects on the Internet, risk being left with only residual space in the global digital networks.

* Many groups such as the Ontario Library Association and the Public Interest Advocacy Centre, which are associated with a participative public culture as opposed to commercial "cultural industries," advocate basic citizenship rights in the emerging communication environment. They stress not just access to the transmission system but access to full participation — and communicative interactivity.

* One key to a democratic, pluralistic and participative information society is a balance of power between systems and infrastructure providers on the one hand and end users on the other. This means decentring control, and locating programming and switching power in the hands of end users.

* Justice Samuel Freedman was an early advocate of the democratization of new technologies because he realized that they are

more than tools; they constitute an environment enabling or disabling individual and community life.

* Technological restructuring for the new economy and designing the layout of the Information Highway are variations on the same issue. It is more than an economic issue. It's a moral and political one.

* The means of communication have become not only the new means of production, but also the new medium of learning, of cultural communication and governance.

* Communication, therefore, has to be designed around an ethic of public service, as well as an ethic of commerce.

* A mixed-model approach to the information society can begin with a discourse on action grounded in the politics of social movements.

QUESTIONS FOR DISCUSSION

There are no answers at this point, only questions we can ask ourselves:

1) Has electronic communication given you a sense of community with other students taking this course? Yes, no, maybe so?
2) Are the electronic communities you're now part of dependent on everyone staying on line, or is it easy to get together face to face? If not, are you worried about that dependency?
3) Do you feel that in gaining new communities in cyberspace, you're losing touch with other communities, and leaving the old ways of communicating behind? Do you feel there's a danger in this?
4) What are the trade-offs between virtual communities (those created through electronic connections) and face-to-face communities?

SOURCES AND FURTHER READINGS

Carey, James, 1989. *Culture as Communication*. Boston: Unwin.

Cruikshank, Jane, 1994. "Community Development: A Way to Recapture the Vision," *Canadian Journal of University Continuing Education* 20(2).

Information Highway Advisory Council, 1995. *Connection, Community, Content: The Challenge of the Information Highway*. Ottawa: Industry Canada.

Johnson, Brian, 1996. "Waiting for Crash," *Maclean's* (November 11).

McMurdy, Deirdre, 1995. "Mighty Mergers," *Maclean's* (August 14).

Menzies, Heather, 1994. "Hyping the Highway," *Canadian Forum* (June).

Reddick, Andrew, 1995. *The Information Superhighway: Will Some Canadians be Left on the Side of the Road?* Ottawa: Public Interest Advocacy Centre.

Reddick, Andrew, 1995. *Sharing the Road: Convergence and the Canadian Information Highway*. Ottawa: Public Interest Advocacy Centre.

Shade, Lesley Regan, 1994. "Computer Networking in Canada: from CA*net to CANARIE," *Canadian Journal of Communication* 19, pp. 53-69.

CHAPTER 11

FEMINIST AND ECOLOGICAL PERSPECTIVES

OVERVIEW

This is the end of the journey. It's appropriate therefore to return to the realm of values and ideas, because the possibilities for Canada and for society in the era of the global village depend on more than the structures of political economy and of cultural representation associated with it. They rest on a dialectic of interaction between structures, people and ideas. In this unit we'll return to the theme posed by many of the thinkers, and artists, discussed earlier in the course: namely the importance, and difficulty, of thinking about technology in a frame larger than itself — larger than the logic of technique. Think of the visual art and literature reviewed in Unit 6. Remember the artists' concern about technology dwarfing people, and threatening our humanity through its scale, its pace and its imposing disciplines. Think of Ursula Franklin's concern that the house of technology we increasingly inhabit is designed with control and compliance in mind. Think of Marshall McLuhan's witty juxtapositions, his constant efforts to make people critically aware of the massaging power of our programmed media environments. Think too of George Grant's lament for the loss of any horizon for thinking and acting in society outside that of instrumental rationality.

Today, philosophers like Jean-François Lyotard speak of data banks as "the new nature" from which we draw the raw materials to make and remake our world. Everything from the workshop and office to the classroom, the living room and even, via cyber-sex, the bedroom is modelled into being by the wrap-around media of digital communication networks. Even the body is represented through these media. People become subjects through texts and form communities through digital connections. Some argue that people are leaving the living world and the living body completely behind. "We are cyborgs. The cyborg is our ontology; it gives us our politics," Donna Haraway writes.

This unit turns the technology frame around. It returns to the body, and the body of the living planet to critically examine what this might mean. It does so by taking the viewpoint of women. The idea is not that women are outside technology, nor that women represent nature as some pristine ideal to which we can return, outside technology as it were. Everywhere from the ozone layer to the ice sheets covering Antarctica, the planet is a mix of biology and technology, and women are as much a part of it as men. Instead, the idea is to focus on technology as an extension of nature and the living body. Women's technological practice offers some insight into this perspective. Partly this is because women and women's technological practice are particularly evident in activities that sustain life: housework, plus child bearing and caring for sick and aging family members. Reexamining these practices can refresh perspectives on the kind of scale, social relations and technological organization that is appropriate to development defined as survival and life sustaining, rather than development defined as market expansion.

Women's perspective is also useful because women have historically been outside the centres of technology design and control. Traditionally, women have been closer to where technology meets human and non-human nature, and where contradictions between the ideal of technology and its reality become apparent. Women thus offer something of an insider-plus-outsider perspective. This is useful as we live more and more of our lives inside this hybrid environment of manufactured and nature-based life-support systems.

The unit begins by looking at the oldest living economy, after that of nature itself; the household economy. The idea here is to reclaim some perspectives on technology associated with its designs for living. We then look at women's experiences with new reproductive technology and infertility to see how development in a technological sense can also involve underdevelopment from the point of view of women and women's natural fertility. And finally, it looks at the philosophy of eco-feminism and uses it as a platform for rethinking some fundamental ideas about technology and sustainable growth, and communication for a sustainable world.

OBJECTIVES

The aim of this unit is to end the course with some critical questions about what "development" and "technology" can be, particularly in terms of living in the digital and genetically engineered Information Age. At the end of this unit, you should be able to answer the following questions:

1) What lessons for technological design and practice can be drawn from the legacy of household technology?
2) Why is the development of new reproductive and genetic technologies a positive thing for doctors and genetic engineers but potentially a negative thing for women?
3) What might be included in an ecological model of communication, and in a policy geared to support it?

PERHAPS THE BIGGEST QUESTIONS about the global village are not who will build it and who will come, but is it sustainable and what is it sustaining? A market for new multi-media products, systems and services? An increasing dependency on digital communication networks for getting around in the world and getting information, services and a job? That's asking the question from the perspective of the technology itself. Turning the frame around, other questions emerge. These include, will it sustain a diversity of voices, knowledge, cultures and communities? Behind that, there's the larger question: will it sustain life in all its biocultural diversity?

The answer depends on the choice paths associated with the new environment and the values attached to them. If the values favour an open design and a plurality of operational models, this should allow diversity to flourish on its own terms. However, if this new environment for living, working and for self-expression is enclosed too much within a global commercial infrastructure, as community-access cable was (see Unit 9), diversity might be reduced to flavour-of-the-month rhetoric in a monoculture of commodity production/consumption.

So it's important to recognize how much words like development and growth have come to mean economic development and market expansion. To remember other meanings, it's essential to turn the frame around. To conceive of these things through another set of values, you have to step outside the centres of market development and the thinking associated with them. You have to occupy another frame of reference, one associated with spiritual as well as material values. The original meaning of spirit is associated with the breath of life itself (remember Chapter 3: *spirare* means "to breathe" in Latin).

Consider the other economies that existed before the global market economy, and continue to exist, albeit increasingly in its shadow. First there's the "economy" of nature itself, which sustains the global village with air to breathe, water to drink and many "natural" sources of food, clothing and shelter. Its value is beyond reckoning, although some have put a multi-billion dollar value on it all. Then there's the economy of the household which sustains life from day to day and from one generation to the next. Recent feminist economists have tried to put a rough dollar figure on its value, and have concluded that it represents the largest single segment of the Canadian economy. But it's largely invisible because its labour is voluntary (even involuntary) and its "products" are eaten or otherwise used in the home, rather than bought and sold outside it.

Household economics has been marginalized in our market-oriented culture. (Think of cultural monopolies of knowledge at work here.)

Yet it is the original economy, and more extensive and longer-lived than the global market economy. The word "economy" itself reveals this fact; it's derived from the Greek word *oekos,* for household. Interestingly, the word "ecology" derives from the same word.

Ellen Swallow Richards (1842-1911), who was the first woman to earn a degree from the Massachesetts Institute of Technology, coined the word ecology ("oekology" as she first used it) to describe a new science dealing with the relations of organisms within their environment. She devoted her life to studying and teaching about healthful environments. (Clarke, 1973)

So household technological practice, geared to sustaining life, not markets, should offer some instructive ideas for technological practice in a global village geared to sustaining life in all its natural and cultural diversity, not just a diversity of multimedia rhetoric.

The first thing to notice here is that the household and family, which can be interpreted to include close friends and relatives, are the central organizing units. The context, then, is not anonymous markets and market relationships, but known people and engaged personal relationships (setting the table; making the salad; cleaning up afterward). Because it's a living context, its scale is small, geared to these living relationships.

Household technology is scaled accordingly. Historically, a lot of this technology was hand made, and embodied that mix of knowledge and material practice that distinguished native technology discussed in Unit 3. By and large, this has changed today, in favour of technology that is purchased, complete with owner manuals. The small scale remains, as does the notion of end-user control of the technology. However, as the infrastructure (or technostructure) for producing household technology has shifted from a range of local craft-scale sites (coopers, sawmills, blacksmiths) to a few remote manufacturing centres, personal and local autonomy has been largely replaced by dependency. A lot of knowledge and improvisational skill has died out of local households at the same time, replaced by prescriptive, patented knowledge and know-how in industrial corporations.

Personal involvement with the technology and the work to be done with it has also long been a hallmark of household technological practice. It's evident in everything from making cheese, beer or bread in the 19th century, to composting, gardening and preserving in the 20th century. With that involvement, knowledge was conserved as it was passed on from one generation to the next, and also renewed with changing times and circumstances.

By and large too, household technological practice has been holistic rather than prescriptive, with family members improvising as they worked, responding to each other's changing needs, and pacing themselves according to present priorities.

The discussion of monopolies of knowledge in Unit 10 can shed some critical insight into why household technological practice is not valued as much as industrial production, nor given much consideration as a possible model of technological practice in the global village. The market-development frame of reference (what can be sold, exported) and the commodity terms of reference have been "hegemonized" to the point that it seems like dreaming to speak of designing the village of global digital communication from a micro-cosmic perspective: from the viewpoint of household economics, so that household end users can sustain themselves materially, socially and culturally through these networks.

But it's a thought.

Farm women and their technology.
National Museum of Science and Technology

WOMEN, INFERTILITY AND THE NEW REPRODUCTIVE TECHNOLOGIES The discussion of household economics and related technological practice provides insight into other possible models for the global village. The feminist critique of the new reproductive technologies (NRTs) highlights the critical importance of perspective: between sustaining life in its spontaneous diversity versus sustaining technology. First, a word of clarification: the new reproductive technologies generally refer to genetic engineering. But because this requires sperm and ova, it includes other activities where women's eggs are being removed from their bodies and can then be used for other purposes. The term, therefore, includes everything from drugs controlling fertility to fetal screening for sex and possible genetic abnormalities, to in-vitro fertilization, artificial insemination and actual genetic manipulation or gene therapy.

Three themes in the feminist discourse are important to consider here. The first two, control through the technology plus dependency, relate to a critique of the NRTs, and those adjunct technologies that foster and sustain the continuing use of NRTs. The third theme, personal autonomy, relates to "the view from here": sustaining natural fertility and personal autonomy.

The first theme arises partly through the global or international scope of the feminist critique of NRTs. Individual women using individual technologies, such as birth-control pills or in-vitro fertilization, are invited to see them as tools of personal choice and liberation. And indeed, they have been used in this way, albeit with difficulties. However, the same companies that are pushing these technologies in so-called developed countries, are also pushing drugs for population control in so-called third-world countries, and using women there to test new drugs (Tudiver, 1993:74).

The issue of control through technology also emerges for women using in-vitro fertilization as a treatment for infertility. This treatment at its simplest involves removing eggs from a woman's ovaries at the point in her menstrual cycle when they are ready to be released for possible insemination. The eggs are then mixed with a man's sperm in a petri dish (hence, "in vitro" which means, in glass) and are cultured there for possible conception. Then the live embryo or embryos are inserted through the cervix into the woman's uterus where they might, or might not, implant themselves in the wall of the uterus and grow to full-term babies.

The themes of control through technology, and related dependency, emerge in a number of ways here. First, hospitals and clinics offering these treatments control who will or will not be admitted. Lesbian and single women have commonly been excluded. Second, the doctors take control of women's lives to varying degrees, sometimes insisting that they take drugs to stimulate their ovaries — drugs which have some dangerous and unknown side effects. Yet the women often feel they have no choice but to comply with the doctors' orders because their infertility leaves them dependent (Menzies, 1993:5). Feminists have challenged this dependency and the related societal assumption that becoming a biological mother is central to a woman's identity. In-vitro fertilization might be an extension of a woman's womb and sense of self. But at the same time, the woman can become an extension of a larger technological system controlled by doctors and technicians and their specialized language, and glamorized by the media.

Surrogacy, or contractual child bearing, also illustrates the control theme, and the exploitation of women as prostitutes is a classic historical precedent. The fear is that women with limited economic choices can be too easily used by the corporate interests already emerging in this field in the US.

The control/dependency theme rings the loudest in the area of genetics itself. This includes, first, genetic screening, which involves using various probes and related tools to diagnose a possible disease or unwanted trait (predisposition to alcoholism and depression being two cited in the research literature). The second area is actual intervention, either using tissue grown by a transgenic mouse or other life form genetically altered for this purpose, or in outright "gene therapy."

Feminists are concerned that women's bodies may be used in this research without commensurate control. But their biggest concern is the transfer of control over human life itself to the hands of doctors and geneticists. There are enormous issues here, from the possibilities of discrimination (what some call "molecular racism") to the myriad forms of intervention. Already, in some jurisdictions in the US, health insurance companies require women policy holders to submit to genetic screening for Down's Syndrome. Already, too, women over 35 are automatically considered problem pregnancies and are urged to submit to genetic screening and counselling.

The technologies that fragment and decontextualize reproduction are changing what it means to bear a child. There are new social relations, new sites of activity, and new sources of power and control.

When you turn the frame around, the central issue for women is autonomy: the freedom and capacity to have children on their own terms. A core issue, therefore, is preventing infertility and preserving women's natural fertility. For example, the most common reason for in-vitro fertilization for infertile women is blocked fallopian tubes. This is most often caused by scarring from pelvic inflammatory disease due to sexually transmitted diseases. In other words, a good deal of infertility in women is preventable. Feminists have called for programs and policies to promote better public health and education to eliminate sexually transmitted diseases. Feminists also call for good, public child-care so that women can have their children when they are younger and more naturally fertile.

The autonomy issue also involves biological diversity, or the capacity to bear life in all its natural, and unpredictable, diversity. This depends on a world view that values life equally as opposed to one that only values life in terms of a prescribed ideal of the perfectibility of man, the perfectibility of the human genome, and the desirability of certain traits over others.

In the video, I talked about my own personal experience with infertility and how coming to terms with that loss had paradoxically renewed my sense of being part of the living earth and its webwork of interconnected life. The experience of fellow feeling for the topsoil being scraped away to make way for yet another housing or industrial-park development was indicative. Nature is no longer outside of me, an abstraction I observe through the lens of culture. It's inside me, a deeply felt presence. It has become a grounding place for thinking about sustaining natural life as compared to sustaining the technological extensions and amputations of life: the cyborg. It's a perspective associated with eco-feminism.

- **E**very year, 24 billion tons of topsoil are lost to erosion; partly because of this, global food production has declined since 1984.
- **E**very five minutes a major shipment of toxic chemicals crosses an international boundary to be disposed of somewhere with little or no environmental-protection legislation.
- **E**very minute, between 20 and 40 hectares of tropical forest are destroyed.
- **E**very year, at least 20,000 species disappear forever. The rate of extinction is accelerating. (Suzuki, 1994:18)

ECOFEMINISM Eco-feminism is a philosophy that integrates the ideas and ideals of feminism with a model of life associated with ecology, the study of the relationship of organisms and their environment. As such it bridges the dichotomy between culture and nature, because it seeks to model culture on nature. Ecology is similar to native science, as discussed in Unit 3, in that it views nature as a webwork of living relationships, not as inert resources over which one species, humanity, has dominion.

Feminism contributes a philosophy that is grounded in the value of equality rather than hierarchy, and an ethic of peaceful coexistence and reciprocity rather than competition and conflict. Eco-feminism's integrated, embodied philosophy is also in contrast to a dichotomizing approach to life (self/other; culture/nature; mind/matter; male/female), which is so central to the mastering ethic associated with technological development for its own sake.

Some of the principles of eco-feminism are:

1) that human beings are part of nature, not apart from it. This changes everything, including the concept of what sustainability is all about: sustaining the environment that sustains all life, or sustaining the techno-environment of market development that sustains the life of commerce.

2) that everything is related to everything else, across time and across space. In genetics, this speaks to the need to honour genetic continuity and the boundaries between species.

3) that there are no real boundaries between the public sphere and the private sphere, between productive work and reproductive work. In economics, this speaks to the need to critically revalue work carried on in the private sphere of the home, and under the rubric of "consumption" and "reproduction."

4) that there are no real boundaries between the personal and the political. This means that what happens personally and locally is a microcosm of the larger whole. It also means that change can happen at the level of personal technological practice, that people have agency. They can act in ways that go beyond the personal.

COMMUNICATIONS TO SUSTAIN LIFE AND A LIVING CULTURE The point of returning to broad principles of philosophy in this chapter, and using feminist perspectives as a point of reference, is to end the journey of this course with some critical questions about culture and identity in the age of digital communications.

Eco-feminism, with its reminders of the differences in world view between First Nations and European approaches to science and technology, provides a framework for thinking about technology in terms beyond itself. Such a framework effectively shifts the discussion agenda from technology-centred questions, such as equitable access to technology, to environment-centred questions, such as opportunities to sustain a diversity of life and culture using whatever technologies are appropriate.

As Ursula Franklin and Langdon Winner have argued, technologies both symbolize and embody a particular social order through the values built into their design and application (see Unit 2). Certain values, philosophies and world views lead development down certain choice paths. Given the development of global corporations and the waning of social institutions that define life in terms larger than production and consumption, the choice paths of the global village could narrow into what eco-feminist Vandana Shiva calls a global monoculture: a self-contained digital simulacrum rather like a Disney World with multiple choice roles orchestrated by Microsoft and other systems providers.

The possibility of negotiating the design of the global village as well as the activities within it depends on critically assessing alternatives in terms of values, such as the material values of space versus the spiritual and ecological values associated with time; alternatives in terms of social relations, such as prescriptive and hierarchial versus holistic and reciprocal; and alternatives in terms of communication models.

Economist and communication theorist, Robert Babe, has broken some important ground in articulating a possible ecological model of communication. As he puts it, it's a model that moves from alienation to wholeness, from entropy to sustainability, and from individualism to person in community.

His contrasting of economics with ecology is critical here. He criticizes the core assumption of economics that people are autonomous individuals driven to maximize their interests. As he elaborated in the video interview, when economics informs the dominant model of communication in society, it channels it narrowly toward "a commodity mode of communication." Buyers and sellers of information meet anonymously in the transactional matrix of the price system, then go their separate ways. No relationships are developed, no social bonds are formed or meaningfully sustained beyond the production and satisfaction of commoditized desires.

This model lends itself to alienation because of the anonymity and fragmented solitariness of the individual exchange. It lends itself to entropy because market economics treats everything from people to nature in strictly commodity terms to be used and inevitably used up. There is no place for renewal in this model; no place for the living whole of the community and the eco-system.

An ecological model of communication replaces the classical economic assumption of individualism with an assumption of relatedness: that communication is about relationships. Furthermore, relationships are the medium through which people constitute themselves as communities and societies. In other words, instead of the mechanistic man-made medium of the price system, the core medium of communication is people in what Babe calls "radical inter-dependency" with each other.

> "In [Adam] Smith's vision, individuals are viewed as capable of relating themselves to others in diverse ways, basically either in benevolence or in self-love, but they are not constituted by these relationships or by any others.... Their relations are external to their own identities.... This picture of human beings is profoundly erroneous. People are constituted by their relationships. We come into being in and through relationships and have no identity apart from them."
> (H. Daly and J. Cobb, 1989:161)

This model is similar in many ways to the community-building social-bonding model of communication discussed in Unit 10. However, it broadens the community frame to include the largest community and source of continuity and bonding: the living earth itself.

Babe argues that communication has largely been transformed into a species of economics, but that this is leading to a crisis of entropy and alienation. He also argues that if economics can itself be transformed by the principles of communication, which in nature involves continuity, radical interdependency and reciprocity, the result would essentially be an ecological model of communication (Babe, 1995:108-15).

In the interview we speculated about what might be included in such a model of communication, and talked about human scale and human pacing, as opposed to the nanosecond speeds of computer-communication. Such a model would also favour present and local control over planned and remote control.

One can also speculate about the kind of policy questions that would be asked, and the kind of technological choice paths that would be opened through this model of communication. Where the core question was sustaining life and human relationships in all their bio- and cultural diversity, the questions would be very different.

There is much critical thinking to be done.

FINAL QUESTIONS

The global village is still under construction. The critical thing is to be aware of it as a social construct, embodying values and world views in its infrastructures and operating systems. One purpose of this course is to promote critical thinking about the global digital networks that are increasingly the site of economic and cultural activity. Hopefully, it has equipped you to explore some critical questions and even engage in them as citizens as well as scholars. Questions such as:

1) Is tele-learning in danger of sustaining the technologies of digital communication at the expense of the culture of engaged learning? What policies could help promote the development of tele-learning as an extension or expression of an ecological model of communication?

2) How would an ecological model of communication differ from the dominant economics or commodity model of communication?

3) What kind of transportation and communication policies would be important to sustain household economics and local environments?

COMMENTARY ON SUPPLEMENTARY READINGS

1) Gwynne Basen, "Following Frankenstein: Women, Technology and the Future of Procreation."

There is an overarching point being made in this reading: namely the influence of myths in our society, and how they push certain narrative lines and technological choice paths over others. Here, Basen is highlighting the male procreative dream epitomized in Mary Shelley's cautionary fable of Dr. Victor Frankenstein whose dream of creating a human being out of dead matter entirely through his genius leads to the destruction of the lives of all he loves around him. Basen quotes from a leading scientist in the field of in-vitro fertilization because she senses an echo of this same lone-male hubris. Related to this are a number of points:

* NRTs such as IVF are developing in a society with gender, class and racial biases.

* These power imbalances are accentuated by the high profile that doctors and scientists developing these technologies command in the mainstream media. In their frame of reference, the questions of risk and ethics raised by feminists are marginalized or trivialized.

* Ethical issues are turned into technical problems with a technical solution — e.g. "fetal harvesting."

* Issues are also removed from public discussion through the technique of fragmentation.

* Through the accumulation of fragmented interventions, procreation is being redefined. It's also being taken out of the hands of women and men in the privacy of their relationships, and put into the hands of scientific experts.

* Basen worries at this shift, not just in terms of personal power but for the implications it has for total remote control over procreation. One implication is the loss of the unknown and unknowable; the literal, as opposed to imagined or figurative, reality is all there is.

* Another problem is the discontinuities of human relationships, and what this means for our culture when a child is born not out of an intimate sexual bonding but a series of fragmented acts and transactions.

2) Maria Mies and Vandana Shiva, "Introduction" to *Ecofeminism.*

This is a brief but useful overview both of eco-feminism itself and the context out of which the need for such a philosophy emerged. In particular:

* This book attempts to make visible the things being made invisible by the commoditizing lens of globalization.

* The authors name identity and difference as the platform for resisting patriarchal capitalism with its imperative dynamic of fragmentation and homogenization.

* An eco-feminist framework of analysis helps to identify the integrated nature of capitalism and patriarchy, and how they meet in the twin exploitation of nature and of women, and the less powerful in general.

* This lens also sees that science and technology are not gender neutral.

* Resistance must be based on an agenda of survival, sustaining life in all its diversity, on its own terms.

* It's hard to cultivate a common front of resistance because of the pervasive world view that divides, separates and subordinates, and treats difference as "other" and turns both into "enemy."

* These dominant ideologies are based on a false consciousness that nature is antagonistic and based on competitive species self-interest, when in fact nature functions on interdependence.

* In rethinking these archetypal images, we also need to rethink fundamental concepts such as freedom; from freedom from nature to freedom within nature and natural necessities of life.

* Similarly, the "catching up" strategy of development is as false and wrong for so-called underdeveloped countries as it is for women.

* Globalization tends to mean the global domination of local and particular interests by a global corporate sector. It is, in fact, the antithesis of what global peace and stability require, once you unmask the rhetoric being used to support globalization.

* The authors warn against the trajectory associated with postmodernism's preoccupation with language and culture to the exclusion of the economic material base of life. Similarly, they worry at its rejection of the universalisms of modernity in favour of "cultural relativism" where basically anything goes, including female genital mutilation. This leaves the universalisms of the global corporate agenda with no critical scrutiny, and ignores the common ground associated with women and men around the world trying to survive.

* Eco-feminism emerged out of three movements: the feminist, peace and ecology movements.

* It makes connections, such as those between patriarchal violence against women, other people and nature, and between the "conquest" of women and the ritual stages of war.

* It's grounded on the idea that everything is connected and related to everything else, and we are united by a deep need for wholeness.

* This also means that the spiritual aspect is not apart from the material. It is immanent (all life and living is sacred), not transcendant.

* It abolishes the opposition and alienation between spirit and matter. It's grounded in the politics of everyday life, not transcendant grand plans and ideologies. Its theory and practice are unified in its subsistence perspective.

SOURCES AND FURTHER READINGS

Babe, Robert E., 1995. *Communication and the Transformation of Economics: Essays in Information, Public Policy and Political Economy.* Boulder: Westview Press.

Basen, Gwynne, 1994. "Following Frankenstein: Women, Technology and the Future of Procreation," in *Misconceptions: The Social Construction of Choice and the New Reproductive and Genetic Technologies*. G. Basen, M. Eichler and A. Lippman, eds. Maple Pond, Ont.: Voyageur Publishing.

Clarke, Robert, 1973. *Ellen Swallow: The Woman who Founded Ecology.* Chicago: Follett Publishing.

Corea, Gena, 1986. *The Mother Machine: Reproductive Technologies from Artificial Insemination to Artificial Wombs*. New York: Harper and Row.

Cowan, Ruth Schwarz, 1983. *More Work for Mother: The Ironies of Household Technology from the Open Hearth to the Microwave*. New York: Basic Books.

Daly, H. and Cobb, J., Jr., 1989. *For the Common Good.* Boston: Beacon Press.

Menzies, Heather, 1993. "Testtube Mothers Speak," *Canadian Forum* (July/August).

Mies, Maria and Shiva, Vandana, 1993. *Ecofeminism*. Halifax: Fernwood.

Shiva, Vandana, 1993. *Monocultures of the Mind.* London: Zed Books.

Suzuki, David, 1994. *A Time to Change*. Toronto: Stoddart.

Tudiver, Sari, 1994. "Canada and the Global Context of the New Reproductive Technologies: A Cautionary Essay," in *Misconceptions: The Social Construction of Choice and the New Reproductive and Genetic Technologies*. G. Basen, M. Eichler and A. Lippman, eds. Maple Pond, Ont.: Voyageur Publishing.

Waring, Marilyn, 1988. *If Women Counted: A New Feminist Economics*. New York: HarperCollins.

CHAPTER 12

REVIEW AND FINAL COMMENTS

This chapter is meant as a guide to reviewing this material in preparation for a final exam or assignment. It might be helpful to re-read the introductory chapter and reassess the purpose of the text and complementary videos: it is to cultivate a critical understanding of Canada as it has been formed, and is currently being shaped, through key technologies — particularly the infrastructures of communication. The text has introduced you to a number of concepts to inform that critical understanding. It has also provided many examples of technological developments, the social forces affecting them and the social effects these have had. As you review all that detail, keep in mind that the aim is to illustrate the concepts at work in these technological systems, in all their social complexity, not so much to recite history. If you can use these concepts to better understand the political economy of industrial-age Canada, and the cultural impact of existing communication media, then these critical thinking tools should help you critique the structural and institutional forces at work today in building the global digital economy and the global cultural village.

Go through the text again and take note of all the concepts. These terms have been highlighted in bold face in the text in the instance where they are defined. It's not essential to memorize these definitions word for word. The important thing is to grasp the key idea or ideas involved: For instance, the key differences between prescriptive and holistic technology concern how things are done. It may be done through a fixed formula or prescribed set of instructions or it may be with the creative conception combined with execution of the action. A second important difference lies in how the technological practice is controlled; remotely or by the technology user.

Another way to consolidate your understanding of these concepts and ideas is to apply them in different contexts. The text, the videos and the required readings provide many examples: contingency or technological development paths, rigidities in the corporate operations of the fur trade and industrial development; the transmission model of communication versus the social-bonding model. Test your understanding of the various concepts and ideas by coming up with your own examples and illustrations. Don't stop with just an item on a list; for instance, CNN, or on-line data-base references as an example of a physical monopoly of knowledge. To know that you really understand the concept, you should be able to explain to a friend or fellow student exactly why this illustrates the concept. You have to name the telling detail: that it's CNN's global network of camera people and satellite communications through which it delivers news updates faster than anyone else. As well, online data bases will make information more accessible faster than off-line sources, books on the shelf in libraries you have to visit, etc. Similarly, you have to be able to pick out the telling details of how Berger broke monopolies of knowledge through the way he conducted his inquiry into the MacKenzie Valley Pipeline.

When you go back through the book, take a moment to re-read the boxed quotes as well. Like the elements of each video program I highlighted in the last program, they've been chosen because they summarize or dramatize the deeper themes of the course, not just the static idea of the "bias of space" or the "bias of time." The quotes often illustrate the dynamic notion that values such as market expansionism or conservation and memory are not only built into the infrastructures and institutions of communication; they also build a social order around those values. The quotes often evoke the complexities involved. It is not just the transportation, financing and administrative systems of the Hudson's Bay Company, the Canadian Pacific Railway etc., as institutional agents in Canada's development. It's also the social relations involved, and the world view or philosophy being expressed or resisted. If you can get a feel for the dynamics at work, then the course is really working for you. It's a dialectic dynamic. It involves both the social construction of technological systems and infrastructures, and the shaping power of those technologies once they've become fixed or rigid investments of money, knowledge, people and institutional interests. Then there's the countervailing dynamic among the groups and interests that have been marginalized. Ask yourself, what kind of countervailing, or offsetting influence is still detectable as these people, these groups and these institutional interests use other media to organize, to communicate, and to survive. If you can do that, you've gone well beyond the expectations of this course.

It's enough if you can discuss the implications or meaning of some of these concepts in different contexts: for instance, how the Internet fits the communitarian, social-bonding model of communication, and what is necessary to prevent it being transformed by interests associated more with the transmission model. Another example is how the rigidities of the transnational railway system contributed to regional economic disparities and unequal development across Canada. You can ask how the rigidities of the new digital economy are shaping a new Post-Fordist work environment in which people work as servo-mechanisms of technological systems.

Finally, can you discuss how McLuhan and Grant are similar in their outlook, and how they are different? How are Innis and Franklin similar, and different?

Go back over the questions that were posed at the beginning and end of each chapter. If you can answer these, and feel confident that you know what you're saying when you do, then you've succeeded in taking in and making use of the critical thinking tools offered here.

Printed in the United States
145481LV00001B/3/P

9 780886 293369